K–3

USER'S GUIDE to the

Early
Language &
Literacy
Classroom
Observation

K–3
Research Edition **TOOL**

D1262086

K–3

USER'S GUIDE to the
Early
Language &
Literacy
Classroom
Observation K–3
Research Edition **TOOL**

by

Miriam W. Smith, Ed.D.
Joanne P. Brady, M.Ed.
& Nancy Clark-Chiarelli, Ed.D.

Education Development Center, Inc.
Newton, Massachusetts

·P A U L·H·
BROOKES
PUBLISHING C.®

Baltimore • London • Sydney

is a registered trademark owned by
Paul H. Brookes Publishing Co., Inc.

To contact the publisher: Paul H. Brookes Publishing Co.,
Post Office Box 10624, Baltimore, Maryland 21285-0624
1-800-638-3775; 1-410-337-9580; fax: 1-410-337-8539
www.brookespublishing.com

The *Early Language and Literacy Classroom Observation Tool, K–3 (ELLCO K–3), Research Edition,* is intended for one-time use only and can be purchased in packages of five (under ISBN-13: 978-1-55766-949-0). To order, contact Brookes Publishing Co.

For information on bulk sales, contact Brookes Publishing's Sales Manager at sales@brookespublishing.com, or call Brookes at one of the numbers listed above.

For information on arranging training for the ELLCO K-3, please contact Brookes Publishing Co.

The case studies in this book are based on the authors' experience. Names and identifying details have been changed to protect privacy.

Typeset by Integrated Publishing Solutions, Grand Rapids, Michigan.
Manufactured in the United States of America by
Sheridan Books, Inc., Chelsea, Michigan.

Library of Congress Cataloging-in-Publication Data

Smith, Miriam W.
    User's guide to the early language and literacy classroom observation tool, K–3 (ELLCO K–3) / by Miriam W. Smith, Joanne P. Brady, & Nancy Clark-Chiarelli.—Research ed.
        p.   cm.
    Rev. ed. of: User's guide to the early language & literacy classroom observation toolkit. c2002.
    Includes bibliographical references.
    ISBN-13: 978-1-55766-948-3 (pbk.)
    ISBN-10: 1-55766-948-1 (pbk.)
    1. Language arts (Early childhood)—Evaluation.   2. English language—Study and teaching (Early childhood—Evaluation.   3. Observation (Education method)   I. Brady, Joanne P. II. Clark-Chiarelli, Nancy.   III. Smith, Miriam W. User's guide to the early language & literacy classroom observation toolkit.   IV. Title.
    LB1139.5.L35S55 2008
    372.6—dc22   200802576

British Library Cataloguing in Publication data are available from the British Library.

2012   2011   2010   2009   2008

10   9   8   7   6   5   4   3   2   1

Contents

About the Authors

Miriam W. Smith, Ed.D., Consultant, Education Development Center, Inc. (EDC), 55 Chapel Street, Newton, Massachusetts 02458

Dr. Smith has always enjoyed working directly with young children and teachers of young children. Beginning in 1987, she collected and analyzed data for the longitudinal Home–School Study of Language and Literacy Development. Her work on that project brought her into many classrooms as an observer and researcher and propelled her interest in classroom environments and practices that promote children's early language and literacy development. Later work conducted for the Center for Children & Families at EDC cemented her commitment to working directly with teachers, supervisors, and education leaders to promote conditions that positively affect children's learning. Currently a consultant to EDC, Dr. Smith continues to engage in research, writing, and professional development with teachers of young children. An active volunteer in local schools and child care programs, she most enjoys spending time in the "living lab" of daily life with her three children.

Joanne P. Brady, M.Ed., Vice President and Director, Center for Children & Families, Education Development Center, Inc., 55 Chapel Street, Newton, Massachusetts 02458

Ms. Brady is recognized nationwide for her contributions to the field of early childhood education. She provides leadership to a range of complex projects that focus on research, assessment, technical assistance, and professional development that translates research and recommended practice into useful programs and products for practitioners and policy makers. Her groundbreaking work with the National Board for Professional Teaching Standards has led to a performance-based assessment to certify accomplished early childhood teachers. In recent years, Ms. Brady has concentrated her efforts on the design of professional development approaches that build teachers' knowledge and skill in content areas, especially language and literacy. Ms. Brady and her colleagues are examining the impact of literacy-related professional development on teachers' practices and children's learning. Ms. Brady presents her work at major conferences and seminars in the United States and abroad and has contributed to numerous publications, including *Critical Issues in Early Childhood Professional Development* (Zaslow & Martinez-Beck, Paul H. Brookes Publishing Co., 2006).

Nancy Clark-Chiarelli, Ed.D., Principal Research Scientist, Center for Children & Families, Education Development Center, Inc., 55 Chapel Street, Newton, Massachusetts 02458

Dr. Clark-Chiarelli began her career as a special education teacher with a specialization in language and literacy development. Over the years, she taught all grades K–12 and has deep knowledge of effective classroom pedagogy. Dr. Clark-Chiarelli is the Principal Investigator on a project studying the impact of two variations of professional development for early childhood educators in the area of language and literacy. Drawing upon her extensive experience in K–12 special education and literacy, Dr. Clark-Chiarelli is also leading a project to identify and study schools with effective K–3 reading programs. In addition to research, her work at Education Development Center, Inc., has also included designing a web site for PBS Parents focused on language and literacy development of children birth through age 8 and numerous online literacy courses for teachers of prekindergarten through sixth grade.

Acknowledgments

The Early Language and Literacy Classroom Observation Tool, K–3, Research Edition, is built on a body of work undertaken at the Center for Children & Families at Education Development Center, Inc. (EDC), from 1997 onward. When the ELLCO Toolkit, Research Edition, was published in 2002, it represented substantial contributions from many staff. In particular, the current authors want to thank David K. Dickinson, who was instrumental in the development of the initial ELLCO, for his efforts and many contributions. Thanks also to Louisa Anastasopoulos, who prepared the Technical Appendix for the original ELLCO Toolkit.

Over the intervening years, many early childhood practitioners and researchers have used the ELLCO across the country. Their feedback and suggestions have helped to guide the creation of the ELLCO K–3. Specifically, we appreciate the thoughtful comments and careful reviews provided by Julie Hirschler and Gail Bolte. We also thank Jean Foley for her support in producing the manuscript and her unflagging attention to detail. Finally, we appreciate the editorial support and encouragement received from the Paul H. Brookes Publishing Co. team throughout the revision process. Many thanks to Heather Shrestha, Editorial Director; Astrid Zuckerman, Acquisitions Editor; and Mika Smith, Editorial Supervisor.

Finally, we wish to thank the many teachers and literacy coaches who welcomed us into their schools and classrooms over the years. Their openness and insights have been critical to the development process.

Introduction
to the ELLCO K–3

The ELLCO was first published in 2002 as the Early Language and Literacy Classroom Observation (ELLCO) Toolkit, Research Edition (Smith & Dickinson, 2002). It was originally designed to observe and rate the quality of language and literacy instruction in both prekindergarten and primary-grade classrooms. This early instrument was composed of items mostly applicable to prekindergarten classrooms, with few items geared to the practices and approaches used in early reading and writing instruction. From careful examination of the literature, contributions from users in the field, and experience working in primary school settings, the Early Language and Literacy Classroom Observation Tool, K–3 (ELLCO K–3), Research Edition, has been devised expressly for use in kindergarten through third-grade settings. The ELLCO K–3 complements the ELLCO Pre-K (Smith, Brady, & Anastasopoulos, 2008) and the Child and Home Early Language and Literacy Observation (CHELLO) Tool (Neuman, Dwyer, & Koh, 2007). The ELLCO Pre-K is available for use in center-based classrooms for 3- to 5-year-old children. The CHELLO has been developed for use in family child care and other home-based settings. Together, these instruments provide practitioners and researchers with tools that describe the extent to which students at different stages of development are receiving optimal support in specific settings for their language and literacy development.

Because the ELLCO K–3 differs substantially from the previous ELLCO Toolkit, it is currently published as a research edition. Although there are studies planned to test its reliability and validity, they are not yet complete. The architecture of the ELLCO K–3 and its content, however, are informed by the use of and research conducted on the ELLCO Toolkit, Research Edition. Following is a review of the literature that forms the basis for many of the items contained in the ELLCO K–3. In addition, there is a technical report for the ELLCO Toolkit, Research Edition, in this user's guide as a reference.

RESEARCH LITERATURE BASE FOR THE ELLCO K–3

The importance of early literacy has been underscored by several seminal reports, such as the report of the National Research Council, *Preventing Reading Difficulties in Young Children* (Snow, Burns, & Griffin, 1998), which highlights the importance of balanced, comprehensive literacy programs. Similarly, the National Reading Panel issued a report, *Teaching Children to Read* (National Institute of Child Health and Human Development [NICHD], 2000), that articulated the effectiveness of various approaches to teaching to read in grades K–6. Yet, despite the fact that research has shown us how to teach students to read, many still are not succeeding. An estimated 20% of our nation's students experience significant difficulty learning to read, and another 20% do not read fluently enough to read for pleasure (Fletcher & Lyon, 1998; Shaywitz, Escobar, Shaywitz, Fletcher, & Makuch, 1992). Results from the National Assessment of Educational Progress (NAEP; National Center for Education Statistics, 2007) indicated that 34% of fourth graders read at a basic level and an additional 33% of fourth graders are considered to be below a basic level. When disaggregated by race/ethnicity, results reveal a vast discrepancy among white, black, and Hispanic students—although 43% of white students read at or above the proficient level, only 14% of black students and 17% of Hispanic students read at these levels (National Center for Education Statistics, 2007).

To address these long-standing disparities in educational achievement, the No Child Left Behind Act (NCLB) of 2001 (PL 107-110) provided new opportunities and challenges for schools and their teachers to ensure academic excellence for all students. A cornerstone of NCLB is accountability. Specifically, in the area of reading/language arts, states have been required to

- Establish statewide standards and assessments aligned with those standards in reading/language arts...

- Assess all students in [G]rades 3–8 in reading/language arts annually by 2005–2006...

- [Develop] assessments [that are] valid, reliable, [and] consistent with relevant, nationally recognized professional and technical standards (Palmer & Coleman, 2003, p. 3)

In an era in which such accountability in reading achievement is paramount, the ELLCO K–3 provides an effective way for practitioners, researchers, and others concerned with quality improvement to gauge progress and focus their program improvement efforts. Moreover, the conceptual framework of the ELLCO K–3 is based on what is known about the components of early reading and writing and effective instruction.

Key Components of Early Reading

Language and literacy are inextricably linked (Adams, 1990; Dickinson & Tabors, 2001; Silliman & Wilkinson, 1994). Students who begin school with a strong language base, including a strong vocabulary and ability to engage in extended discourse, have an academic advantage over their peers (Hart & Risley, 1995; Snow et al., 1998). Regardless of the skills and language proficiency students bring to their first school experience, much can be done in the classroom to facilitate students' oral language development (Wilkinson & Silliman, 2000). Explicit instruction in vocabulary (Beck, Perfetti, & McKeown, 1982; NICHD, 2000; Wixson, 1986), incidental instruction in vocabulary (Blachowicz & Fisher, 2000; NICHD, 2000), and providing students with plenty of opportunity to practice using extended discourse through classroom conversations (Cazden, 1988; Wells & Chang-Wells, 2001) are all effective ways to facilitate students' language and literacy growth. Students for whom English is a second language and students who are linguistically diverse benefit from careful assessment, scaffolding, and support (Cummins, 1989; Reed & Railsback, 2003; Wilkinson & Silliman, 2000) in the classroom.

Underlying the ability to work with the alphabetic system is the capacity to hear and manipulate sounds in words. Therefore, phonemic awareness should be emphasized for young children, particularly before they have much familiarity with print (Adams, 1990; Moats, 2000; Snow et al., 1998; Torgesen, Morgan, & Davis, 1992; Williams, 1980). Once students have begun to learn sound–symbol associations and the alphabetic principle, writing and invented spelling support students' ability to identify and manipulate sounds in words (NICHD, 2000; Richgels, 2001; Torgesen, Wagner, & Rashotte, 1997).

In order to "unlock the code" of written language, beginning readers need instruction in sound–symbol association that is explicit and systematic (Adams, 1990; Byrne & Fielding-Barnsley, 1989; Chall, 1987; A.E. Cunningham, 1990; Ehri, 1991; Ehri & Chun, 1996; Foorman, Francis, Fletcher, Schatschneider, & Mehta, 1998; Snow et al., 1998) and that provides sufficient practice in applying graphophonemic strategies to text, particularly to connected text (P.M. Cunningham & Allington, 2002; Stahl & Duffy-Hester, 1998). Different methods of phonics instruction can be equally effective as long as they are systematic (Chall, 1987; NICHD, 2000; Stahl, 2001).

As students develop into readers, there is the need for automatic identification of sight words and proficient sound–symbol association (Adams, 1990; Ehri, 1991; Snow et al., 1998). They also need to be able to read text fluently (LaBerge & Samuels, 1974; Samuels, 1994) in order to allocate cognitive resources necessary for the comprehension of text (Kuhn & Stahl, 2000; NICHD, 2000; Rasinski, 2004; Samuels, 2002). Moreover, methods of instruction that effectively foster greater fluency in students have been clearly identified (Rasinski, 2004; Samuels, 2002). Specifically, instructional methods that emphasize the use of modeling of fluent reading (Chomsky, 1976; Eldredge, 1990; Labbo & Teale, 1990) and repeated reading (Morris & Nelson, 1992; Samuels, 1979; Samuels, Schermer, & Reinking, 1992) have been shown to be effective in increasing students' fluency.

Because comprehension is the ultimate goal of reading, young readers need to become aware of their own thinking—metacognition—and be able to apply the invisible strategies that good readers use as they construct meaning from text (Brown, Bransford, Ferrara, & Campione, 1983; Deschler & Schumaker, 1988; Duffy, Roehler, & Hermann, 1988). Key comprehension strategies include making connections to background knowledge, predicting, summarizing, clarifying, making inferences, and using visualization (Pearson & Fielding, 1991; Pressley, 1994).

Research and practice suggest that effective beginning reading instruction

- Emphasizes explicit teaching that models, demonstrates, and explains specific strategies and behaviors used in reading connected text (Bereiter & Bird, 1985; Palincsar & Brown, 1984; Pressley et al., 1991)

- Provides students opportunities to practice new strategies with teacher support that is aligned with their abilities (Beed, Hawkins, & Roller, 1991; Tharpe & Gallimore, 1988; Vygotsky, 1934/1986)

- Carefully matches readers to texts, considering both text difficulty and students' interests (Berliner, 1981; Chall, Bissex, Conrad, & Harris-Sharples, 1996; Chall & Conard, 1991; Gambrell & Morrow, 1996)

- Varies the difficulty of text, depending on the type of reading activity or instruction (Fountas & Pinnell, 1999; Gunning, 1998). For example, optimally during independent reading, students read text at their independent level. But, during teacher-supported instruction, text should be more challenging.

- Uses strategies to create flexible, small groupings of students with similar levels of reading proficiency (Taylor, Pearson, Clark, & Walpole, 1999)

- Frequently monitors progress in order to regroup students, based on teacher observation (Keisling, 1978; Slavin, Stevens, & Madden, 1988; Taylor et al., 1999)

Key Components of Early Writing

Since the 1980s, the emphasis in writing instruction has shifted from a focus on product to a focus on process. Experts such as Graves (1987) and Calkins

(1994) argued that students should learn to write using the same processes that skilled writers use—that is, by writing about topics that interest them and by revising their work multiple times. This process approach to writing has been conceived of as having distinct stages: brainstorming, drafting, revising, editing, and publishing—each requiring different skills (Calkins, 1994). To implement the process approach, many have recommended that large blocks of time be set aside for workshops in which students write (Calkins, 1994). Just as skilled writers rely on feedback and collaboration from others, even the youngest students benefit from peer input (Calkins, 1994; Graves, 1987).

Bromley (1999) outlined five components of writing instruction that are generally accepted in the literature:

- Standards and assessment should guide writing instruction.

- Teachers should provide large blocks of time for writing, talking, and sharing.

- Students should receive direct instruction in composing and conventions.

- Students should have a choice in writing topics and write for a variety of purposes and audiences.

- Writing should be used across the curriculum to construct meaning.

Although there is limited research on effective writing instruction to date, existing literature does support a process approach to writing instruction, indicating that student achievement in writing is superior when writing instruction is process oriented rather than product oriented (Cotton, 2004). In fact, results from NAEP assessments indicate that students who were expected to write multiple drafts of papers scored significantly better than those who were expected to turn in only a finished product (National Center for Education Statistics, 1999).

ORGANIZATION OF THE ELLCO K-3

The ELLCO K-3 consists of an observation instrument and a teacher interview designed to supplement the observation. The observation contains a total of 18 items, organized into five main sections:

- Section I: Classroom Structure contains four items that address classroom organization and contents, management practices, and professional focus.

- Section II: Curriculum consists of three items that address the integration of language and literacy, opportunities for independence in learning, and recognition of diversity.

- Section III: The Language Environment includes three items that focus on the discourse climate in the classroom, opportunities for extended conversations, and efforts to build vocabulary.

- Section IV: Books and Reading contains five items that address the characteristics of books available and the development of the key components of reading: reading fluency, phonics and phonemic awareness, vocabulary, and comprehension.

- Section V: Print and Writing includes three items that focus on the writing environment, writing instruction, and students' writing products.

The ELLCO K–3 is scored and tabulated so that there are two main subscales. Sections I and II combine to create the *General Classroom Environment* subscale. Sections III, IV, and V join together to create the *Language and Literacy* subscale. These subscales are intentionally differentiated, with the emphasis placed on the *Language and Literacy* subscale, which contains the majority of items (11), whereas the *General Classroom Environment* subscale includes the remaining 7 items.

UNDERLYING ASSUMPTIONS OF THE ELLCO K–3

The ELLCO K–3 is based on several central assumptions about the nature of students' literacy development and the conditions and opportunities in classrooms that either support or detract from such development:

- Opportunities to use and practice oral language and literacy skills are fostered in classrooms that are structured to support students' initiative, actively engage students in learning experiences, and blend goals for other content areas with literacy learning.

- Teachers are responsible for instructing students in the key components of literacy that teach and reinforce appropriate reading and writing development.

- Teachers have a responsibility to understand, evaluate, and respond appropriately to individuals' differing literacy skills and learning needs.

- Connections are made among students' oral language use, the opportunities students have to engage in extended talk, and their developing capacities as readers and writers.

- Decisions about classroom organization, provision of materials, and scheduling of time are made thoughtfully, with the intent of fostering language, literacy, and learning.

- Teachers plan curricula that support students in developing their language, reading, and writing proficiencies while engaging them in cognitively challenging learning.

- Teachers use a range of assessment techniques to evaluate learning and adjust their instruction accordingly.

WHO SHOULD USE THE ELLCO K–3?

The developers of ELLCO K–3 recommend that potential users have strong background knowledge of students' language and literacy development as well as experience teaching in primary-grade classrooms. Furthermore, they should understand how instruction adjusts to the changing capacities of students as the students move from kindergarten to third grade. A range of professionals may be interested in using the ELLCO K–3 for a variety of purposes, including the following:

- Researchers who are engaged in evaluating the quality of language and literacy practices in primary-grade classrooms

- Curriculum coordinators and literacy coaches, who are involved in supporting the development of teachers

- Professional development facilitators, interested in fostering a shared vision of effective language and literacy instruction, who want to use a tool that provides both a springboard for discussion and a means for systematic documentation of progress

- Teachers who are interested in a tool that stimulates their assessment and reflection on their classroom practices and strategies

HOW DOES THE ELLCO K–3 COMPARE WITH THE ELLCO TOOLKIT, RESEARCH EDITION?

Thanks to the widespread use of the original ELLCO Toolkit, Research Edition, and feedback from a diverse body of users, we have incorporated a range of changes in the creation of this new instrument. These changes serve to make the ELLCO K–3 easier to use and score and more focused than the original ELLCO. For users familiar with the original ELLCO, it is important to note that items from the Literacy Environment Checklist[1] and Literacy Activities Rating Scale now have been integrated into the architecture of the ELLCO K–3 observation itself (see further details on these items in the technical report). The purpose of this substantial change was to make several of the observation items more robust by including details previously gathered by the Literacy Environment Checklist and the Literacy Activities Rating Scale and reduce reliance on counting literacy materials and activities that tended to skew results. For instance, classrooms with more materials, regardless of whether or how they were used, were more likely to receive higher ratings. The ELLCO K–3 explicitly values *how* materials are used by teachers and students more than whether materials are merely present. The most significant change is the specificity and depth of items that gauge evidence-based approaches linked to effective reading and writing instruction. This version also includes detailed descriptive indicators at each of the five scale points (rather than for just three), which will help observers more clearly and reliably decide how to rate each item. Chapter 3 provides more details on the structure of ELLCO K–3 tool.

CONTENTS OF THE USER'S GUIDE

The remaining chapters of this user's guide provide detailed support to enable practitioners and researchers to understand how to score the ELLCO K–3 and use it for different purposes.

- Chapter 2, "Effective Elements of Early Literacy: Kenny's Story," uses a series of vignettes of a first-grade student's experiences in the classroom to illustrate key components of early literacy. It also demonstrates the way that everyday events can be translated into evidence to support ratings of ELLCO K–3 items.

- Chapter 3, "Structure of the ELLCO K–3," addresses the content of each section, the architecture of items, and the contents of the Teacher Interview.

- Chapter 4, "How to Conduct an ELLCO K–3 Observation," offers specific guidelines for scheduling and preparing for a classroom visit, general strategies for rating items, ways to avoid bias in scoring items, and considerations for classrooms at different grade levels.

- Chapter 5, "A Review of Sample Items," walks the user through steps in rating three different items. Classroom vignettes, sample evidence, and

---

[1]The Literacy Environment Checklist will continue to be made available by Brookes Publishing. See http://www.brookespublishing.com/ellco for details on obtaining the Literacy Environment Checklist. This will enable grantees to supply the U.S. Department of Education with the necessary data required by the Government Performance and Results Act of 1993 (PL 103-62).

explanatory text simulate how an observer translates what was seen and heard into scores for specific items.

- Chapter 6, "Using the ELLCO K–3 for Professional Development," discusses how the instrument itself and various components of the user's guide can be used as an effective vehicle for promoting teacher reflection and collective responsibility for student learning. It offers guidelines for building the ELLCO K–3 into ongoing professional development and provides practical ideas tied to each of the five sections of the tool.

- Chapter 7, "Using the ELLCO K–3 in Research," describes the characteristics of effective data collector training, including criteria for selecting observers, approaches to achieving and calculating interrater reliability, and recalibrating observers in the field.

The user's guide concludes with two appendixes. The first is a technical report that describes data gathered with the ELLCO Toolkit, Research Edition, and outlines how these data informed the creation of the two separate tools, the ELLCO Pre-K and the ELLCO K–3, Research Edition. A second appendix is devoted to a variety of resources, including an annotated set of web sites, articles, and books that are relevant to early literacy research and instruction.

REFERENCES

Adams, M.J. (1990). *Beginning to read: Thinking and learning about print.* Cambridge, MA: MIT Press.

Beck, I.L., Perfetti, C.A., & McKeown, M.G. (1982). Effects of long-term vocabulary instruction on lexical access and reading comprehension. *Journal of Educational Psychology, 74*(4), 506–521.

Beed, P.L., Hawkins, M.E., & Roller, C.M. (1991). Moving learners toward independence: The power of scaffolded instruction. *The Reading Teacher, 44,* 648–655.

Bereiter, C., & Bird, M. (1985). Use of thinking aloud in identification and teaching of reading comprehension strategies. *Cognition and Instruction, 2,* 91–130.

Berliner, D.C. (1981). Academic learning time and reading achievement. In J. Guthrie (Ed.), *Comprehension and teaching: Research reviews* (pp. 203–225). Newark, DE: International Reading Association.

Blachowicz, C.L., & Fisher, P.H. (2000). Vocabulary instruction. In M.L. Kamil, P.B. Mosenthal, P.D. Pearson, & R. Barr (Eds.), *Handbook of reading research* (Vol. III, pp. 503–523). Mahwah, NJ: Lawrence Erlbaum Associates.

Bromley, K. (1999). Key components of sound writing instruction. In L.B. Gambrell, L.M. Morrow, S.B. Neuman, & M. Pressley (Eds.), *Best practices in literacy instruction* (pp. 152–174). New York: Guilford Press.

Brown, A.L., Bransford, J.P., Ferrara, R.A., & Campione, J.C. (1983). Learning, remembering, and understanding. In J.H. Flavell & E.M. Markman (Eds.), *Handbook of child psychology: Vol. 3. Cognitive development* (pp. 177–206). New York: Wiley.

Byrne, B., & Fielding-Barnsley, R. (1989). Phonemic awareness and letter knowledge in the child's acquisitions of the alphabetic principle. *Journal of Educational Psychology, 81,* 313–321.

Calkins, L. (1994). *The art of teaching writing.* Portsmouth, NH: Heinemann.

Cazden, C. (1988). *Classroom discourse: The language of teaching and learning.* Portsmouth, NH: Heinemann.

Chall, J.S. (1987). *Learning to read: The great debate* (Updated ed.). New York: McGraw-Hill.

Chall, J.S., Bissex, G.L., Conard, S.S., & Harris-Sharples, S. (1996). *Qualitative assessment of text difficulty: A practical guide for teachers and writers.* Cambridge, MA: Brookline Books.

Chall, J.S., & Conard, S.S. (1991). *Should textbooks challenge students?* New York: Teachers College Press.

Chomsky, C. (1976). When you still can't read in third grade: After decoding, what? *Language Arts, 53*(3), 288–296.

Cotton, K. (2004). *School improvement research series: Topical synthesis #2. Teaching composition: Research on effective practices.* Portland, OR: Northwest Regional Educational Laboratory. Retrieved October 18, 2007, from http://www.nwrel.org/scpd/sirs/2/topsyn2.html

Cummins, J. (1989). *Empowering minority students.* Sacramento: California Association for Bilingual Education.

Cunningham, A.E. (1990). Explicit versus implicit instruction in phonemic awareness. *Journal of Experimental Child Psychology, 50,* 429–444.

Cunningham, P.M., & Allington, R.L. (2002). *Classrooms that work: They can all read and write* (3rd ed.). Boston: Allyn & Bacon.

Deschler, D.D., & Schumaker, J.R. (1988). An instructional model for teaching students how to learn. In J.O.L. Graden, J.E. Zins, & M.J. Curtis (Eds.), *Alternative educational delivery systems: Enhancing instructional outcomes for all students* (pp. 391–411). Washington, DC: National Association of School Psychologists.

Dickinson, D.K., & Tabors, P.O. (Eds.). (2001). *Beginning literacy with language: Young children learning at home and school.* Baltimore: Paul H. Brookes Publishing Co.

Duffy, G., Roehler, L., & Hermann, B. (1988). Modeling mental processes helps poor readers become strategic readers. *The Reading Teacher, 41,* 762–767.

Ehri, L.C. (1991). Learning to read and spell words. In L. Rieben & C.A. Perfetti (Eds.), *Learning to read: Basic research and its implications* (pp. 57–73). Mahwah, NJ: Lawrence Erlbaum Associates.

Ehri, L.C., & Chun, C. (1996). How alphabetic/phonemic knowledge facilitates test processing in emerging readers. In J. Shimron (Ed.), *Literacy and education: Essays in memory of Dina Feitelson* (pp. 69–93). Cresskill, NJ: Hampton Press.

Eldredge, J.L. (1990). Increasing the performance of poor readers in the third grade with a group-assisted strategy. *Journal of Educational Research, 84*(2), 69–77.

Fletcher, J.M., & Lyon, G.R. (1998). Reading: A research-based approach. In W. Evers (Ed.), *What's gone wrong in America's classrooms?* (pp. 49–90). Stanford, CA: Hoover Institution Press.

Foorman, B.R., Francis, D.J., Fletcher, J.M., Schatschneider, C., & Mehta, P. (1998). The role of instruction in learning to read: Preventing reading failure in at-risk children. *Journal of Educational Psychology, 90,* 37–55.

Fountas, I.C., & Pinnell, G.S. (1999). *Matching books to readers: Using leveled books in guided reading. K–3.* Portsmouth, NH: Heinemann.

Gambrell, L.B., & Morrow, L.M. (1996). Creating motivating contexts for literacy learning. In L. Baker, P. Afferbach, & D. Reinking (Eds.), *Developing engaged readers in school and home communities* (pp. 115–136). Mahwah, NJ: Lawrence Erlbaum Associates.

Graves, D.H. (1987). *Writing: Teachers and children at work.* Portsmouth, NH: Heinemann.

Gunning, T.G. (1998). *Best books for beginning readers.* Boston: Allyn & Bacon.

Hart, B., & Risley, T.R. (1995). *Meaningful differences in the everyday experience of young American children.* Baltimore: Paul H. Brookes Publishing Co.

Keisling, H. (1978). Productivity of instructional time by model of instruction for students at varying levels of reading skills. *Reading Research Quarterly, 13,* 554–582.

Kuhn, M.R., & Stahl, S.A. (2000). *Fluency: A review of developmental and remedial practices* (CIERA Rep. No. 2-008). Ann Arbor: University of Michigan, Center for the Improvement of Early Reading Achievement. Retrieved May 18, 2004, from http://www.ciera.org/library/reports/inquiry-2/2-008/2-008.pdf

Labbo, L.D., & Teale, W.H. (1990). Cross-age reading: A strategy for helping poor readers. *The Reading Teacher, 43,* 363–369.

LaBerge, L.D., & Samuels, S.J. (1974). Toward a theory of automatic information processing in reading. *Cognitive Psychology, 6,* 293–323.

Moats, L.C. (2000). *Speech to print: Language essentials for teachers.* Baltimore: Paul H. Brookes Publishing Co.

Morris, D., & Nelson, L. (1992). Supported oral reading with low achieving second graders. *Reading Research and Instruction, 32,* 49–63.

National Center for Education Statistics. (1999). *NAEP 1998 writing: Report card for the nation and the states* (NCES 1999-462). Washington, DC: Author. Retrieved October 18, 2007, from http://nces.ed.gov/pubsearch/pubsinfo.asp?pubid=1999462

National Center for Education Statistics. (2007). *The nation's report card: Reading 2007. National Assessment of Educational Progress at Grades 4 and 8* (NCES 2007-496). Washington, DC: Author. Retrieved October 18, 2007, from http://nces.ed.gov/nationsreportcard/pdf/main2007/2007496.pdf

National Institute of Child Health and Human Development (NICHD). (2000). *Report of the National Reading Panel. Teaching children to read: An evidence-based assessment of the scientific research literature on reading and its implications for reading instruction. Reports of the subgroups* (NIH Pub. 00-4754). Washington, DC: U.S. Government Printing Office. Also available online: http://www.nichd.nih.gov/publications/nrp/upload/report_pdf.pdf

Neuman, S.B., Dwyer, J., & Koh, S. (2007). *Child/Home Early Language and Literacy Observation (CHELLO) Tool.* Baltimore: Paul H. Brookes Publishing Co.

No Child Left Behind Act of 2001, PL 107-110, 115 Stat. 1425, 20 U.S.C. §§ 6301 *et seq.*

Palincsar, A.S., & Brown, A.L. (1984). Reciprocal teaching of comprehension-fostering and comprehension-monitoring activities. *Cognition and Instruction, 2,* 117–175.

Palmer, S.R., & Coleman, A.L. (2003). *Summary of NCLB requirements and deadlines for state action.* Retrieved January 10, 2007, from http://www.ccsso.org/content/pdfs/Deadlines.pdf

Pearson, P.D., & Fielding, L. (1991). Comprehension instruction. In R. Barr, M.L. Kamil, P.B. Mosenthal, & P.D. Pearson (Eds.), *Handbook of reading research* (Vol. II, pp. 815–860). New York.

Pressley, M. (1994). Transactional instruction of reading comprehension strategies. In J. Manfieri & C. Block (Eds.), *Creating powerful thinking in teachers and students* (pp. 113–139). Fort Worth, TX: Harcourt Brace College.

Pressley, M., El-Dinary, P.B., Gaskins, I., Schuder, T., Bergman, J.L., Almasi, J., et al. (1991). Beyond direct explanation: Transactional instruction of reading comprehension strategies. *The Elementary School Journal, 92,* 513–555.

Rasinski, T. (2004). Creating fluent readers. *Educational Leadership, 61*(6), 46–51.

Reed, B., & Railsback, J. (2003). *Strategies and resources for mainstream teachers of English language learners.* Retrieved April 16, 2004, from http://www.nwrel.org/request/2003may/ell.pdf

Richgels, D.J. (2001). Invented spelling, phonemic awareness, and reading and writing instruction. In S.B. Neuman & D.K. Dickinson (Eds.), *Handbook of early literacy research* (pp. 142–155). New York: Guilford Press.

Samuels, S.J. (1979). The method of repeated readings. *The Reading Teacher, 42,* 220–226.

Samuels, S.J. (1994). Toward a theory of automatic information processing in reading, revisited. In R.B. Ruddell, M.R. Ruddell, & H. Singer (Eds.), *Theoretical models and processes of reading* (4th ed., pp. 816–837). Newark, DE: International Reading Association.

Samuels, S.J. (2002). Reading fluency: Its development and assessment. In A.E. Farstrup & S.J. Samuels (Eds.), *What research has to say about reading instruction* (3rd ed., pp. 166–183). Newark, DE: International Reading Association.

Samuels, S.J., Schermer, N., & Reinking, D. (1992). Reading fluency: Techniques for making decoding automatic. In S.J. Samuels & A.E. Farstrup (Eds.), *What research has to say about reading instruction* (2nd ed., pp. 124–144). Newark, DE: International Reading Association.

Shaywitz, S.E., Escobar, M.D., Shaywitz, B.A., Fletcher, J.M., & Makuch, R.W. (1992). Evidence that dyslexia may represent the lower tail of a normal distribution of reading ability. *New England Journal of Medicine, 326,* 145–150.

Silliman, E.R., & Wilkinson, L.C. (1994). Discourse scaffolds for classroom intervention. In G.P. Wallach & K.G. Butler (Eds.), *Language learning disabilities in school-age children and adolescents* (pp. 27–54). Boston: Allyn & Bacon.

Slavin, R.E., Stevens, R.J., & Madden, N.A. (1988). Accommodating student diversity in reading and writing instruction: A cooperative learning approach. *Remedial and Special Education, 9,* 60–66.

Smith, M.W., Brady, J.P., & Anastasopoulos, L. (2008). *Early Language and Literacy Classroom Observation Tool, Pre-K (ELLCO Pre-K).* Baltimore: Paul H. Brookes Publishing Co.

Smith, M.W., & Dickinson D.K. (with Sangeorge, A., & Anastasopoulos, L.). (2002). *Early Language and Literacy Classroom Observation (ELLCO) Toolkit* (Research ed.). Baltimore: Paul H. Brookes Publishing Co.

Snow, C.E., Burns, M.S., & Griffin, P. (Eds.). (1998). *Preventing reading difficulties in young children.* Washington, DC: National Academies Press.

Stahl, S.A. (2001). Teaching phonics and phonological awareness. In S.B. Neuman & D.K. Dickinson (Eds.), *Handbook of early literacy research* (pp. 142–155). New York: Guilford Press.

Stahl, S.A., & Duffy-Hester, A.M. (1998). Everything you wanted to know about phonics (but were afraid to ask). *Reading Research Quarterly, 33,* 338–355.

Stahl, S.A., Heubach, K., & Crammond, B. (1997). *Fluency-oriented reading instruction* (Reading Research Report No. 79). Athens, GA: National Reading Research Center.

Taylor, B.M., Pearson, P.D., Clark, K.F., & Walpole, S. (1999). *Beating the odds in teaching all children to read* (CIERA Report #2-006). Ann Arbor: University of Michigan, Center for the Improvement of Early Reading Achievement.

Tharpe, R.G., & Gallimore, R. (1988). *Rousing minds to life: Teaching, learning, and schooling in social context.* New York: Cambridge University Press.

Torgesen, J.K., Morgan, S., & Davis, C. (1992). Effects of two types of phonological awareness training on word learning in kindergarten children. *Journal of Educational Psychology, 84,* 364–370.

Torgesen, J.K., Wagner, R.K., & Rashotte, C.A. (1997). Prevention and remediation of severe reading disabilities: Keeping the end in mind. *Scientific Studies of Reading, 1,* 217–234.

Vygotsky, L.S. (1986). *Thought and language* (Rev. ed., E. Hanfmann & G. Vakar, Trans., A. Kozulin, Ed.). Cambridge, MA: MIT Press. (Original work published 1934)

Wells, G., & Chang-Wells, G. (2001). The literate potential of collaborative talk. In B.M. Power & R.S. Hubbard (Eds.), *Language development: A reader for teachers* (pp. 155–168). Upper Saddle River, NJ: Prentice-Hall.

Wilkinson, L.C., & Silliman, E.R. (2000). Classroom language and literacy learning. In M.L. Kamil, P.B. Mosenthal, P.D. Pearson, & R. Barr (Eds.), *Handbook of reading research* (Vol. III, pp. 337–360). Mahwah, NJ: Lawrence Erlbaum Associates.

Williams, J.P. (1980). Teaching decoding with an emphasis on phoneme analysis and phoneme blending. *Journal of Educational Psychology, 72,* 1–15.

Wixson, K.K. (1986). Vocabulary instruction and children's comprehension of basal stories. *Reading Research Quarterly, 21*(3), 317–329.

Effective Elements of Early Literacy

Kenny's Story

Using the ELLCO K–3 gives educators and researchers a concrete way to examine the literacy-related features of classrooms. One of the goals of the ELLCO K–3 and its user's guide is to help educators in the early elementary grades (kindergarten through third grade) improve the quality of the literacy and language learning taking place in their classrooms by providing a better understanding of which practices promote such learning. Kenny's Story can help teachers and observers grasp the context for and importance of observing and rating literacy-related practices and materials in a classroom. Kenny's Story also can function as a starting point from which teachers brainstorm ways to improve their own practices and foster students' experiences with language and print. It can be used either after the ELLCO K–3 has been completed or while teachers engage in professional development.

The vignettes that follow and the corresponding ELLCO K–3 items are not intended to be an exhaustive picture of an ELLCO K–3 observation. Instead, they are illustrative of the types of activities and exchanges one might see when visiting an early elementary school classroom, and in this case, a first-grade classroom. These vignettes, extracted from Kenny's day, offer a picture of where evidence for rating ELLCO K–3 items may be observed within the regular course of classroom events.

Vignette 1: Entering

> "Mrs. Porter! Mrs. Porter! Look what I found!" screamed Kenny as he bounded into his first-grade classroom, proudly holding up a snakeskin for his teacher to see. "Whoa, Kenny! It's nice to see you so excited this morning, but I need you to slow down just a bit. I tell you what, honey, just as soon as you hang your things up and sign in on the board, we can take a look at that discovery together." Kenny hurried over to his labeled coat hook, removed some crumpled papers and a brown bag from his backpack, tossed the backpack on the ground, and hung his sweatshirt on the hook. Then he raced to a nearby bin to deposit his lunch bag, careened around the corner to place his homework in a file box labeled "Mrs. Porter's In-Box," and quickly scribbled his name at the bottom of the list on the blackboard. "Okay!" Kenny shouted, "I'm ready now!" "Great," replied Mrs. Porter, "let's take a look and see what this amazing thing is."

Kenny is a first-grade student in a large, urban elementary school entering his classroom on a typical day. He greets his teacher with enthusiasm and a discovery that he is clearly excited about, and she greets him warmly in return. His teacher reminds him gently of the daily check-in procedures, which he accomplishes quickly and independently, due in part to the organization of the classroom, which includes labeled bins and boxes, accessible writing tools, and a well-defined, familiar sequence of actions that he can readily accomplish. A classroom environment that is intentionally structured to support students' independence fosters a sense of belonging and their ability to affect their own learning community (Farran, Aydogan, Kang, & Lipsey, 2006; Justice, 2004; Roskos & Neuman, 2001). In addition, participation in regular, systematic literacy routines, such as reading labels and signing names, reinforces students' knowledge of the functions of print and supports their own efforts to create meaningful print (Whitehurst et al., 1994). In an actual ELLCO K–3 observation, evidence from this vignette might support ratings for the following items:

Item 1, Organization of the Classroom

Item 3, Classroom Management

Item 4, Professional Focus

Item 8, Discourse Climate

Vignette 2: Analyzing the Discovery

> Kenny and Mrs. Porter took the snakeskin to the classroom windowsill, where there was a lot of light. There were several small bins of science equipment, including small trays, magnifiers, and tweezers, which they used to manipulate and examine the skin. "Wow, this is so cool!" exclaimed

Kenny as he looked carefully at the skin through a magnifier. "It has like a million tiny squares on it."

"Would you like to do an observational drawing of it before we get going this morning?" inquired Mrs. Porter as she started to move toward the door to greet more of her students. There was a stack of paper and a tin can of pencils nearby, which Kenny used to begin his drawing. After working for several minutes, Kenny wondered aloud, "I wonder what kind of snake it's from." Kenny glanced around the room and then noticed that the shelves beneath the windowsill contained a variety of science reference books, including several books about snakes and reptiles. He abandoned his drawing and turned his attention to the books, quickly finding two books with snakes pictured on their covers: *Why Do Snakes Hiss?* by Joan Holub, and the Level 2 DK Reader, *Slinky, Scaly Snakes* by Jennifer Dussling. Carefully taking his snakeskin, his drawing, and the books, Kenny headed to his seat at a table in his classroom.

Mrs. Porter's first-grade classroom appears to invite students to independently select activities and materials for learning. For Kenny, on this day, the small science area contained materials that he could use to look closely at his snakeskin and writing supplies to help him further his understanding by drawing. When students are offered regular access to writing materials, they are able to explore the functions and forms of writing and with teacher support may begin to write letters, names, words, and short phrases (Schickedanz & Casbergue, 2004). The science materials were complemented by the strategically placed reference books that Kenny, a beginning reader, could access on his own. In this vignette, it is notable that the teacher is nearby to offer support, yet she encourages Kenny to explore and work on his own. Teacher support that is flexible and focused on the needs and interests of students supports their learning (Strickland & Snow, 2002). Once again, Kenny shows his knowledge of classroom routines as he independently takes his snakeskin and works in progress to his table before Mrs. Porter begins the official school day. In an actual ELLCO K–3 observation, evidence from this vignette might support ratings for the following items:

Item 2, Contents of the Classroom

Item 6, Opportunities for Independence in Learning

Item 11, Characteristics of Books

Item 16, Writing Environment

Vignette 3: Reading Group

Later in the morning, Kenny and his small reading group (five students total) gather at a table with Mrs. Porter. She distributes copies of the leveled reader *Where Animals Live* to each student. The books are first-grade level, with three to five words per sentence, five to seven sentences per page, and repeated high-frequency words (e.g., *this, some*). Mrs. Porter directs the students to look at the cover of the book and make a prediction about the subject. When the students finish chiming in their ideas, Mrs. Porter attaches a large piece of paper to an easel and asks the students what they already know about animal homes and whether they can name some specific animal homes. The small group quickly generates a list that includes the following:

tree	house
nest	brick wall
ocean	sewer
hole	hive
cave	

Mrs. Porter then guides the students through their silent and choral reading of the book, acknowledging individual students for their efforts in decoding and reading fluency. Kenny reads the page in the book about animals that live in the water and wonders aloud whether the snake that shed its skin might live in the water. This prompts a brief, lively discussion of the local *urban* environment and whether a water snake would be a likely *inhabitant* of the city streets. Most students think not, although several allow for the possibility that snakes could live in the sewers beneath the streets. After about 25 minutes of small-group reading and talking, Mrs. Porter sends the students back to their seats with a worksheet to be completed. The worksheet includes several key words from the story (*this, these, some, live*) that students use to make their own sentences and drawings about animals and animal homes. Mrs. Porter redirects the students' attention to their word list and tells them to try to use some of these new words as they complete their worksheets. Kenny quickly finishes his worksheet and drawings and delivers them to Mrs. Porter's in-box.

Helping students become readers and writers is an essential task for early elementary grade teachers, who are often faced with students who have varying degrees of knowledge and skill. In this case, it appears that Mrs. Porter has already determined her students' reading levels and is providing instruction in small groups using a series of leveled readers matched to students' interests and her instructional goals. She also makes an effort to include some vocabulary and writing activities that may further supplement and support her students' learning. Teaching vocabulary in the context of book reading is a powerful way to help students connect written words with spoken vocabulary (Justice & Kaderavek, 2002; McKeown & Beck, 2006). Discussing word definitions in the context of reading models ways to develop meaning from texts (e.g., comments such as "What do you think it means?" or "What does the picture show?") and may reinforce students' later efforts in reading comprehension (Biemiller, 2006; Neuman, Snow, & Canizares, 2000). A focus on vocabulary words that connect with the curriculum and are reinforced in displays and used throughout the classroom provides additional support for students' word learning and vocabulary use (Farran et al., 2006; Justice, 2004). In an actual ELLCO K–3 observation, evidence from this vignette might support ratings for the following items:

Item 5, Integration of Language and Literacy

Item 7, Recognizing Diversity in the Classroom

Item 9, Opportunities for Extended Conversations

Item 10, Efforts to Build Vocabulary

Item 12, Development of Reading Fluency

Item 16, Writing Environment

Vignette 4: End of the Day

> At the end of each school day, Mrs. Porter reads aloud to her students from a challenging chapter book. At the time of this observation, the class is midway through *James and the Giant Peach*, by Roald Dahl. As the students lay sprawled about on the classroom carpet and several beanbag chairs, they listen intently to the story. Mrs. Porter reads clearly and with enthusiasm, pausing periodically to glance at the faces of her students and occasionally to answer a question. Despite the difficult vocabulary (*whereupon, dregs, armadillo*), the students seem to be following the narrative and are thrilled when Mrs. Porter reads a passage containing one of the Centipede's silly poems, a large copy of which is already hung in their classroom.
>
> At the conclusion of the reading time, Kenny sighs heavily. Mrs. Porter asks him what's wrong, and he replies "That is just the *best* story! I wish it could go on and on."
>
> Mrs. Porter reaches over and gives Kenny a warm hug and replies, "And it will, Kenny. Tomorrow. But now it's time to get your things and pack up to go home."

In the elementary grades, hearing stories and books read aloud is an important component of language and literacy learning. And in Kenny's classroom, it is also a pleasurable, comfortable ritual among teacher and students that helps them wind down their classroom day and begin their transition toward home. Items from the ELLCO K–3 that might be addressed in this vignette include the following:

Item 5, Integration of Language and Literacy

Item 8, Discourse Climate

Item 15, Strategies to Build Reading Comprehension

Item 16, Writing Environment

Taken together, these vignettes demonstrate emergent literacy in action in a typical first-grade classroom. As Kenny went through his school day, he was offered a variety of ways to explore and expand his knowledge of science, of reading, of writing, and of the culture of school. Kenny's participation in these activities reflects his growing understanding of the functions and nature of reading and writing. He knew where to look for books in his classroom and could identify their topics by pictures and words. He was able to read and understand simple, leveled books. He connected vocabulary words from his reading lesson with a simple writing assignment and enjoyed listening to a complex narrative read aloud. Mrs. Porter's classroom and her teaching style invited Kenny to become a participant in the world of school and the universe of reading and writing.

REFERENCES

Biemiller, A. (2006). Vocabulary development and instruction: A prerequisite for school learning. In D.K. Dickinson & S.B. Neuman (Eds.), *Handbook of early literacy research* (Vol. 2, pp. 41–51). New York: Guilford Press.

Dahl, R. (1961). *James and the giant peach* (Nancy Eckholm Burkert, Illus.). New York: Knopf.

Farran, D.C., Aydogan, C., Kang, S.J., & Lipsey, M.W. (2006). Preschool classroom environments and the quantity and quality of children's literacy and language behaviors. In D.K. Dickinson & S.B. Neuman (Eds.), *Handbook of early literacy research* (Vol. 2, pp. 257–268). New York: Guilford Press.

Justice, L.M. (2004). Creating language-rich preschool classroom environments. *Teaching Exceptional Children, 37*(2), 36–44.

Justice, L.M., & Kaderavek, J. (2002). Using shared storybook reading to promote emergent literacy. *Teaching Exceptional Children, 34*(4), 8–13.

McKeown, M.G., & Beck, I.L. (2006). Encouraging young children's language interactions with stories. In D.K. Dickinson & S.B. Neuman (Eds.), *Handbook of early literacy research* (Vol. 2, pp. 281–294). New York: Guilford Press.

Neuman, S., Snow, C.E., & Canizares, S. (2000). *Building language for literacy.* New York: Scholastic.

Roskos, K., & Neuman, S.B. (2001). Environment and its influences for early literacy teaching and learning. In S.B. Neuman & D.K. Dickinson (Eds.), *Handbook of early literacy research* (pp. 281–292). New York: Guilford Press.

Schickedanz, J.A., & Casbergue, R.M. (2004). *Writing in preschool: Learning to orchestrate meaning and marks.* Newark, DE: International Reading Association.

Strickland, D., & Snow, C.E. (2002). *Preparing our teachers: Opportunities for better reading instruction.* Washington, DC: Joseph Henry Press.

Whitehurst, G.J., Epstein, J.N., Angell, A.C., Payne, A.C., Crone, D.A., & Fischel, J.E. (1994). Outcomes of an emergent literacy intervention in Head Start. *Journal of Educational Psychology, 86,* 542–555.

3

Structure of the ELLCO K–3

OVERALL STRUCTURE AND LEVELS

As described in Chapter 1, the ELLCO K–3 comprises 18 items, grouped into five main sections (see Table 3.1). Each item is designed to capture important and observable aspects of language and literacy in the primary grades. While each item is unique in its focus, all items are uniform with respect to their structure.

Each item is constructed to describe the characteristics of classroom practice at five distinct levels, from *exemplary* to *deficient*, with the highest number indicating the most accomplished level of performance. Therefore, Level 5 indicates *exemplary* practice; Level 4 indicates *strong* practice; Level 3 indicates *basic* practice; Level 2 indicates *inadequate* practice; and Level 1 indicates *deficient* practice.

Each item consists of anchor statements for each level, as well as descriptive indicators, which are provided as scoring guidance for each item. An evidence page is provided for each item, to allow for detailed recording of pertinent evidence observed during the classroom visit. The following sections discuss the anchor statements, descriptive indicators, and evidence pages in further detail.

The ELLCO K–3 also includes a Teacher Interview, a brief and supplementary component of the classroom observation, and a score form for summarizing and totaling scores. The Teacher Interview is discussed briefly in this chapter. Chapter 4 provides detailed information on conducting an observation and interview and using the score form.

Table 3.1. Structure of the ELLCO K-3, Research Edition

GENERAL CLASSROOM ENVIRONMENT

Section I: Classroom Structure

Item 1: Organization of the Classroom

Item 2: Contents of the Classroom

Item 3: Classroom Management

Item 4: Professional Focus

Section II: Curriculum

Item 5: Integration of Language and Literacy

Item 6: Opportunities for Independence in Learning

Item 7: Recognizing Diversity in the Classroom

LANGUAGE AND LITERACY

Section III: The Language Environment

Item 8: Discourse Climate

Item 9: Opportunities for Extended Conversations

Item 10: Efforts to Build Vocabulary

Section IV: Books and Reading

Item 11: Characteristics of Books

Item 12: Development of Reading Fluency

Item 13: Sounds to Print

Item 14: Strategies to Build Reading Vocabulary

Item 15: Strategies to Build Reading Comprehension

Section V: Print and Writing

Item 16: Writing Environment

Item 17: Focused Writing Instruction

Item 18: Students' Writing Products

ANCHOR STATEMENTS

Associated with each level is an anchor statement that has been devised for each item. The intent of this overarching statement is to capture the essence of the practice that is being rated and the nature and quality of evidence required to assign a particular score. While each item demands different content, anchor statements across all items have a consistent element. At each scale point, the orienting language contains a key word, in boldface, to signal the strength of evidence required to assign that score.

- All *exemplary* items begin with the phrase, "There is **compelling** evidence . . . "

- All *strong* items begin with the phrase, "There is **sufficient** evidence . . . "

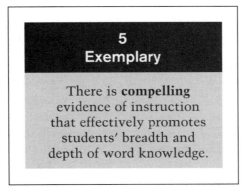

Figure 3.1. Level 5 (*exemplary*) anchor statement for ELLCO K–3, Research Edition, Item 14, Strategies to Build Reading Vocabulary.

- All *basic* items begin with the phrase, "There is **some** evidence . . . "

- All *inadequate* items begin with the phrase, "There is **limited** evidence . . . "

- All *deficient* items begin with the phrase, "There is **minimal** evidence . . . "

This pairing of rating level and key word is intended to help raters differentiate among levels of practice observed. For example, see Figure 3.1 for the Level 5 (*exemplary*) anchor statement for Item 14, Strategies to Build Reading Vocabulary. The anchor statement is critical in determining a rating. It alerts the observer to watch and listen for instructional activities that introduce and reinforce the understanding and use of new words.

DESCRIPTIVE INDICATORS

The anchor statement at each level is followed by a series of bulleted statements, called *descriptive indicators,* which provide more detail about the types and quality of practice that should be observed in order to assign a particular score. It is essential that observers understand that the descriptive indicators are *not* intended to be a checklist. Instead they are guideposts and exemplars that help to distinguish one level from another. If we examine the first descriptive indicator for Item 14, Strategies to Build Reading Vocabulary, we can see that Level 5 (*exemplary*) is characterized by the following description:

> *The teacher creates a climate in which intellectual risk taking is valued, and students are encouraged to experiment with the power of words. The teacher models use of sophisticated vocabulary and chooses texts that make use of challenging words and concepts.*

In comparison, the descriptive indicator for Level 4 (*strong*) suggests a qualitative difference (emphasis added):

> *The teacher creates a climate in which* **students are exposed to and encouraged to try out new words.** *The teacher* **uses challenging** *vocabulary and chooses texts that make use of challenging words and concepts.*

The Level 4 descriptive indicator clearly demonstrates that the teacher is creating an instructional climate in which word knowledge is valued. However, the first descriptive indicator at Level 4 points to two aspects that are different from Level 5, as noted in the boldface italic phrases just mentioned. Observers are guided to notice the extent to which students are supported to experiment with new words and their meanings. In addition, the level of the words introduced and used may be less sophisticated, though appropriately challenging.

As you proceed across levels for the first descriptive indicator of Item 14 to Level 2 (*inadequate*), observers' knowledge about instructional strategies that lead to vocabulary development forcefully comes into play. Level 2 is characterized as follows (emphasis added):

> *Vocabulary instruction is relegated to specific times and* **narrowly prescribed activities,** *thereby* **limiting opportunities** *for students to encounter and use new words. The teacher may appear* **uncomfortable** *using new or challenging vocabulary or may use it* **incorrectly.**

At this level it is clear that the teacher provides limited instruction to build reading vocabulary. Although the teacher may have focused activities that introduce new words, he or she does not model the use of challenging words that build students' understanding of the meaning of new, difficult words.

Taken together, the anchor statement and descriptive indicators represent the qualitative rubric for rating each item. Although these elements are common across items, the nature of the evidence examined and the contents of rubrics are fashioned specifically for each item. Therefore, observers should be very familiar with the rubric before observing a classroom.

EVIDENCE SECTION

In addition, we have added an evidence section for each item. We have provided summary words and/or phrases to help observers quickly and accurately focus their attention on the type of evidence necessary to score the item. For example, for Item 14, Strategies to Build Reading Vocabulary, we direct observers

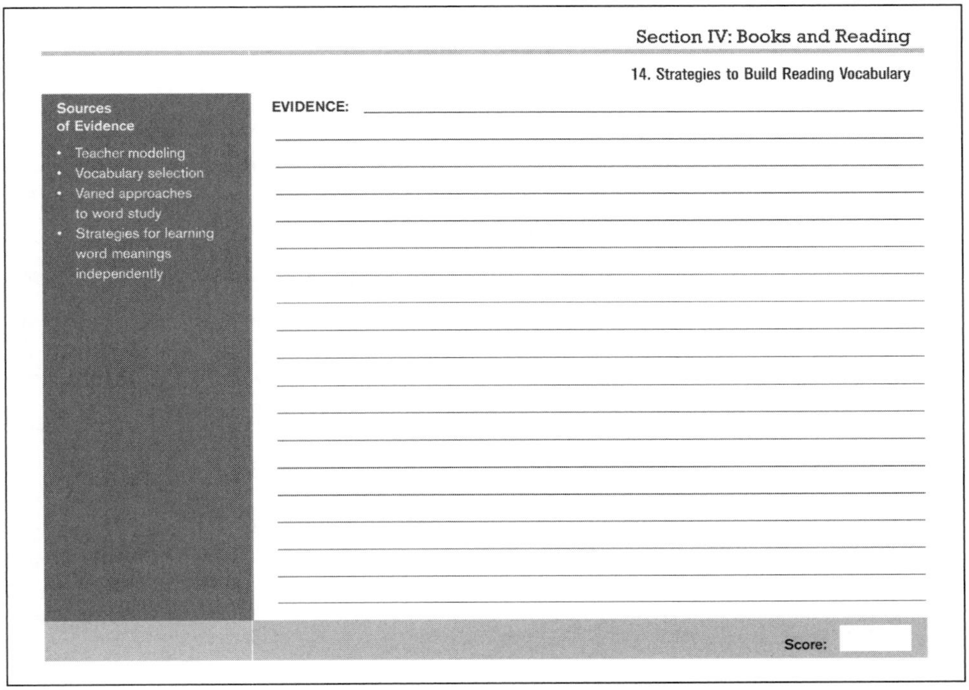

Section IV: Books and Reading

14. Strategies to Build Reading Vocabulary

Sources of Evidence

- Teacher modeling
- Vocabulary selection
- Varied approaches to word study
- Strategies for learning word meanings independently

EVIDENCE:

Score:

Figure 3.2. Evidence section for ELLCO K–3, Research Edition, Item 14, Strategies to Build Reading Vocabulary.

to take data on *teacher modeling, vocabulary selection, varied approaches to word study,* and *strategies for learning word meanings independently* (see Figure 3.2).

TEACHER INTERVIEW

The ELLCO K–3 instrument is followed by a set of brief Teacher Interview questions that can be used to gather information to supplement or provide context for observed data. Interview questions are not to be used as evidence in and of themselves but to elucidate specific aspects of the observation and evidence noted.

How to Conduct an ELLCO K–3 Observation

GUIDELINES FOR OBSERVING IN CLASSROOMS

Scheduling and Duration of Observations

Prior to conducting an ELLCO K–3 observation, contact the classroom teacher to explain the general purpose of your visit. Work with the teacher to choose a day for your visit in order to ensure as typical a picture of the classroom as possible. For example, do not schedule your visit on a day when special activities or visitors are planned. You should also obtain information about the classroom schedule and time your observation accordingly. Allow at least 3.5 hours for your visit to collect ample evidence to score all of the ELLCO K–3 items. Plan to observe for as much of a typical classroom day as possible, particularly reading instruction, writing, and other full- or small-group instructional time. It is important to see teachers interacting with students in various settings in order to get an accurate picture of the instructional environment and the types of conversations that take place between teachers and students and among students.

In addition to selecting the appropriate day and time for your visit, your initial telephone conversation with the teacher can also provide information needed to complete some items on the cover page and Observation Record page. Ask the teacher for information that will enable you to complete background information, such as the district, school, grade, and teacher information; the duration of the classroom day; the age ranges of students and numbers of students with identified disabilities; the number of English language learners; the primary language spoken in the classroom; and languages spoken by

English language learners. The remaining items on the Observation Record page should be completed at the time of the observation.

Conducting Observations with Professionalism and Respect

Classroom observations can be an anxiety-provoking experience for teachers. As the observer, you can help teachers feel more comfortable by taking care to treat them respectfully throughout the entire process. Remember that you are a guest in the classroom. Be sure to greet all teaching staff, introduce yourself, and thank them for allowing you to observe. Remind them how long you plan on staying and indicate that you will do your best to keep out of their way.

Although you will need to position yourself in order to see and hear everything that goes on during your observation, make an effort to be as unobtrusive as possible. In order to ensure that you do not influence what you are trying to observe, you should minimize your impact on the classroom. After your initial greeting, do not interact with the students or the adults, and maintain a neutral facial expression regardless of what you might see or hear during the observation. Students may approach you with questions or comments, but a simple explanation that you are there to see what they are learning and are not able to chat is usually enough to satisfy their curiosity.

Preparing for the Observation

Before conducting an observation, you should carefully read through all of the ELLCO K–3 items several times to familiarize yourself with the content and sequence of the items. Be sure that you thoroughly understand what evidence is needed to rate each item before your visit so that you can focus your attention on the classroom activities during your observation. You may wish to highlight or circle key words and phrases to help you focus on the most important features of each item.

The ELLCO K–3 is a sophisticated observation tool that requires you to use your judgment as a professional who is knowledgeable about primary-grade education as well as early language and literacy practices. It is, therefore, strongly recommended that observers have a background in early childhood education and prior experience conducting classroom observations. Specific ELLCO K–3 training also will help ensure that the tool is administered appropriately. For more information about available training, contact Paul H. Brookes Publishing Co.

TAKING EVIDENCE AND RATING ITEMS

Focusing on the Evidence

Each ELLCO K–3 item rating is based on the evidence you note throughout your observation. What is evidence? Evidence is represented in the notes that describe what you saw and heard in relation to each item. Classrooms are inherently complex places, and recording evidence can be challenging due to the nonlinear nature of classroom life. Observers should be prepared to flip through the tool in order to record evidence in the correct places. To help you focus your observation and note taking, the ELLCO K–3 provides summary phrases that are helpful reminders. For example, for Item 1, Organization of the Classroom, the evidence you should look for includes *independent access to materials and activities, traffic flow for groupings,* and *furnishings* (see Figure 4.1).

There are several items for which evidence can and should be gathered at a time when students are not present in the classroom, either prior to their arrival or during outdoor play. These items all deal with classroom materials, and it will be both easier and less intrusive to examine them when the classroom is empty. The items are

Item 2, Contents of the Classroom

Item 11, Characteristics of Books

Item 16, Writing Environment

Rating Strategies

There are two main strategies that can help you in assigning ratings for the ELLCO K–3 items. One tip that will add structure and focus to your scoring decisions is to start by reading the Level 5 anchor statements and descriptive indicators to determine if you can assign the highest possible score. If the evidence does not support a Level 5 rating, then move on to the Level 4 description. Continue to work your way down until you find the level that best matches the evidence you have noted.

A second strategy is useful when the evidence is mixed or uneven. There may be occasions when a classroom exhibits characteristics that fall under more than one level for a particular item. Using Item 2, Contents of the Classroom, as an example, a classroom may have materials that are organized in conceptually related groups and that are in ample supply, and students may be ob-

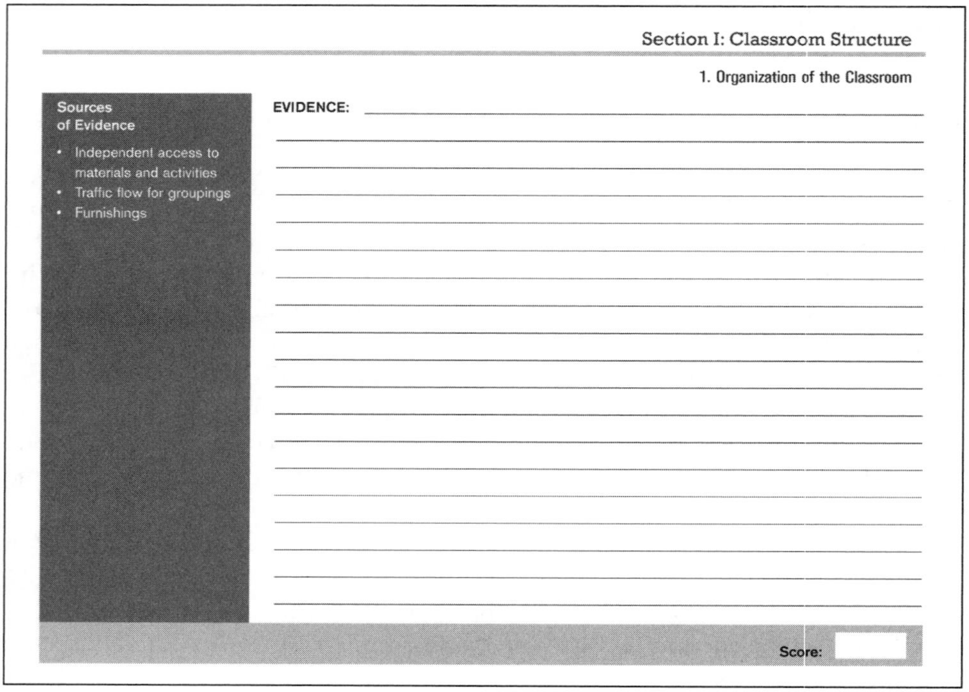

Figure 4.1. Evidence page for ELLCO K–3, Research Edition, Item 1, Organization of the Classroom.

served accessing materials independently (all consistent with Level 4 descriptive indicators), but the classroom's displays may be more teacher-generated than the Level 4 descriptive indicator suggests. In cases such as this one, revisit the anchor statements to guide your scoring. Does the classroom exhibit *sufficient* evidence that the materials are well organized, appealing, accessible, and coordinated with ongoing learning goals? *Some* evidence? *Limited* evidence? Step back from the descriptive indicators and focus on the qualitative anchor statement. Use the evidence you have noted to make your final score determination.

Avoiding Bias

When taking evidence and scoring each particular item, it is important to remain focused on the evidence associated with that item. It is easy for scoring decisions to become clouded by overall impressions of the classroom. A well-stocked and smoothly managed classroom with pleasant teacher–student interactions may predispose an observer to assign higher scores for all of the items, even though there may not be sufficient evidence of effort to build students' vocabulary or engage in extended conversations. Conversely, a teacher with a seemingly disorganized classroom may do a wonderful job with reading instruction, but an observer's view may be negatively influenced by the haphazard classroom environment.

Another factor to guard against during scoring is personal bias. Everyone has opinions of what constitutes a good classroom or teacher. Some of these opinions may coincide with the research-based evidence represented in the ELLCO K–3 items, but other opinions may be irrelevant and solely based on personal preference. The scoring of each item must be based on how the evidence compares with the rubric. It is the observer's job to guard against allowing personal bias to prejudice scoring decisions.

Considering Grade Level and Timing

The ELLCO K–3 spans a wide range of grade levels and potentially an even wider range of student ages. This can present a challenge for observers, who must interpret evidence in light of the particular grade observed. Because exemplary instruction changes from grade to grade, it is vital that qualified observers have practical experience with and knowledge of reading and writing development at *each* grade level.

Although the ELLCO K–3 provides overarching anchor statements and descriptive indicators that encompass what observers might see and hear at each scale point across grades, we have added examples that are intended to illustrate how essential characteristics are instantiated in a classroom. Examples offered in the tool itself are, by necessity, specific to a particular grade level (e.g., kindergarten, third grade). It is critical that observers do not rely on these brief illustrations as a substitute for the actual rubric or their own expertise. For instance, in Section IV: Books and Reading, Item 12, Development of Reading Fluency, gives an example of a third-grade classroom in which the teacher models reading the poem "The Snake," by Emily Dickinson, and then discusses features of the text that guide her reading aloud. Although the construct observed would remain the same at other grades, what would be seen and heard is likely to differ. In a kindergarten classroom, for instance, a text might be selected to familiarize students with common phonemes that support initial decoding in the service of developing fluency (e.g., *Hop on Pop*, by Dr. Seuss). What is important to rating this item is the extent to which the teacher ties the reading selection and the fluency discussion to the appropriate developmental level of the students in the grade observed.

Likewise, in Section V: Print and Writing, observers must also be sensitive to the expected progression of the teaching and learning of writing across the primary grades. Take Item 17, Focused Writing Instruction. Brief examples offered in the Level 5 descriptive indicators suggest a second- or third-grade classroom. Yet, the descriptive indicators are relevant for all grade levels:

- *The teacher provides systematic writing instruction through brief, focused lessons with individuals or groups. They address writing process, mechanics, and use of techniques to achieve particular effects. . . .*
- *Students are observed writing and using a multistep process to advance their writing abilities and sense of themselves as writers. Students plan, draft, revise, edit, or publish during designated writing periods or at times integrated with other content-area blocks.*
- *The teacher talks with students about their writing. The teacher and students explore the intended goals for written assignments and together generate ideas for ways to strengthen writing. . . .*

In a first-grade classroom, a focused lesson on writing might help students develop their own story structure by demonstrating the use of idea webbing. Keep in mind that the ELLCO K–3 provides a research-based framework for rating language and literacy practice across four grade levels. It is not a checklist, nor is the instrument the expert. Instead, the ELLCO K–3 provides the needed architecture to liberate observers' expertise.

Sensitivity to grade level is essential to conducting an ELLCO K–3 observation. It is also important for observers to attend to the time of year in which the observation takes place. For instance, an early fall observation of writing activities will necessarily reveal different levels of expectation, teacher instruction, and student products than those from later in the school year. When rating Item 18, Students' Writing Products, observers should request the opportunity to examine portfolios or other systems that teachers use to collect and organize students' writing products. Observers should apply a reasonable standard to these portfolios and consider the time of year and the grade observed when evaluating the contents.

Finally, observers must be sensitive to the particulars of staffing during observations. This is most relevant to Item 4, Professional Focus. The second descriptive indicator is based on the teacher's "productive involvement" of additional adults, if they are present, in the learning activities of the classroom. There may be occasions when observers see only one teacher with the group of students for the duration of the observation. If this happens, it is acceptable and appropriate for observers to rate Item 4 based only on the first descriptive indicator (the teacher's professional focus). This is noted on the tool.

THE TEACHER INTERVIEW

The Teacher Interview portion of the ELLCO K–3 is designed to provide information to supplement your observation. Interviews should be conducted after you have concluded your observation and during a time when the teacher is free of teaching responsibilities. When you schedule your observation, ask the teacher to set aside time for this brief conversation.

The purpose of the Teacher Interview is twofold. First, the interview allows the observer to gain an understanding of whether the classroom day observed was typical, as indicated by the first question and its probes. This question may become important if the number of students present during the observation differs significantly from the number reported by the teacher prior to your observation. In this way, the observer could determine whether a second visit is required. Second, observers such as supervisors and literacy coaches may be using the ELLCO K–3 as part of an ongoing professional development initiative. In these cases, the additional teacher interview questions help to illuminate teachers' thinking and planning.

Because the interview provides only supplemental information, teacher responses should not be used as direct evidence for scoring determinations. During the interview, a teacher may confirm what you have already observed, thereby increasing your confidence in assigning a particular rating. On the other hand, if the teacher's interview responses contradict what you observed, you should rely on what you saw and noted during your observation to assign the score.

COMPLETING THE SCORE FORM

The ELLCO K–3 Score Form provides space to organize the scores for all 18 of the observed items, allows you to calculate subtotals for each section, and enables you to create two overarching subscale scores, one for the general classroom environment and another specifically for language and literacy.

The 18 ELLCO K–3 items are organized into five sections: Classroom Structure, Curriculum, The Language Environment, Books and Reading, and Print and Writing. After entering the scores for each item in the blank space provided, you can calculate each section's subtotal by taking the sum of all of the items in the section. The highest possible subtotal for each section is as follows:

Section I: Classroom Structure (sum of Items 1–4) = 20

Section II: Curriculum (sum of Items 5–7) = 15

Section III: The Language Environment (sum of Items 8–10) = 15

Section IV: Books and Book Reading (sum of Items 11–15) = 25

Section V: Print and Writing (sum of Items 16–18) = 15

After calculating a subtotal for each of the five sections, you are ready to calculate the two ELLCO K–3 subscales, the *General Classroom Environment* subscale and the *Language and Literacy* subscale. The subscales can be helpful both as a means of structuring feedback to classroom teachers regarding the results from classroom observations and also to measure changes in these two distinct areas. Subscales are arrived at by combining sections as follows:

Section I: Classroom Structure + Section II: Curriculum = *General Classroom Environment* subscale (35 points total)

Section III: The Language Environment + Section IV: Books and Reading + Section V: Print and Writing = *Language and Literacy* subscale (55 points total)

In order to derive a level of proficiency for the classroom when tracking subscales, the observer simply needs to divide the total points assigned for the subscale by the number of items included in it (*General Classroom Environment*

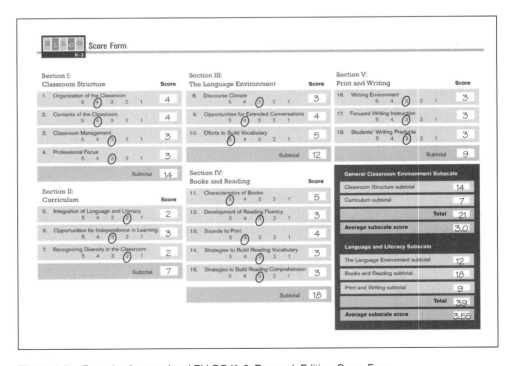

Figure 4.2.   Example of a completed ELLCO K–3, Research Edition, Score Form.

subscale = 7; *Language and Literacy* subscale = 11). This will provide an average rating between 1 and 5, generally corresponding to the rating level key words (e.g., Level 4, *strong*). For example, the *Language and Literacy* subscale shown in Figure 4.2 received a total of 39 points of a possible score of 55 points, divided as follows:

The Language Environment subtotal = 12 points

Books and Reading subtotal = 18 points

Print and Writing subtotal = 9 points

The subscale score (39) divided by number of items in the subscale (11) equals an average score of 3.55. This classroom at this point in time is solidly between *basic* and *strong* for *Language and Literacy* items. By examining the components of the subscale, you can identify particular areas of strength and weakness. In this example, The Language Environment is a relative strength (4.0); whereas Books and Reading (3.6) is somewhat weaker; and Print and Early Writing (3.0) is the weakest. This type of score analysis allows tracking progress over time and offers the ability to more effectively target professional development efforts.

A Review of Sample Items

RECORDING EVIDENCE

Evaluating the quality of evidence is essential to scoring ELLCO K–3 items. Rating accuracy depends on observers noticing and recording ample descriptive evidence relevant to each item. The ELLCO K–3 provides space for documenting the observation and includes key words and phrases that focus observers' attention on sources of evidence. For example, to record evidence for Item 8, Discourse Climate, observers should note the specific details of verbal interactions, including who is participating, the topic, the duration, the affect of teachers and students, and strategies used to facilitate participation and extend interaction. Due to the nature of this item (e.g., based on conversations), it is often helpful to transcribe segments of interaction verbatim in order to capture the flavor and details of the discourse.

UNDERSTANDING THE RUBRICS

Each observation item consists of a rubric with five levels. The anchor statement at each level is most important and should be used as the primary basis for making a scoring decision (see Figure 5.1).

Reading *across* the levels, notice that the phrasing at each level is identical, except for the qualitative words that describe the strength of the evidence (e.g., *exemplary* and *compelling* at Level 5, *strong* and *sufficient* at Level 4).

Reading *within* each level, notice that the anchor statement is followed by a series of bulleted statements that are called descriptive indicators. These *do not* constitute a checklist but are provided to describe in more detail the characteristics of the evidence that might be seen at each scale point (see Figure 5.2).

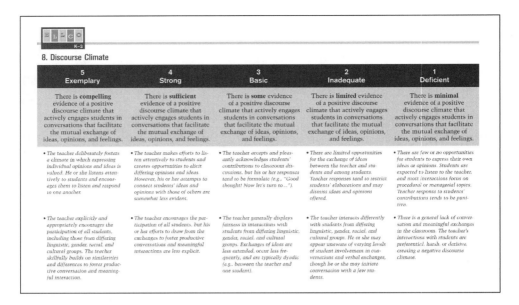

Figure 5.1. Anchor statements (top) and descriptive indicators (bulleted items) for ELLCO K–3, Research Edition, Item 8, Discourse Climate.

In order to rate an item, observers must be familiar with the characteristics of the rubric at each scale point and be able to make qualitative, differential judgments based on what they saw, heard, and recorded. In learning to use the observation tool, it is helpful to notice what changes from level to level.

What changes from Level 5 to Level 4 (see Figure 5.2)? The quality of the evidence observed shifts from *exemplary* and *compelling* to *strong* and *sufficient*. As the descriptive indicators suggest, the teacher may make fewer or weaker efforts to engage multiple students in positive, shared conversations that connect thoughts and ideas, but there are still numerous appropriate and positive interactions. Evidence that the teacher works to involve all students and to deliberately foster further discussion among students is also present but less notable at Level 4 than at Level 5.

What changes from Level 4 to Level 3 (see Figure 5.3)? The quality of what is observed again shifts downward, this time from *strong* and *sufficient* to *basic* and *some*. Indicators at Level 3 describe generally positive interactions that fairly accept and acknowledge students' contributions; however, strategies do not appear to intentionally engage students in making connections with one another's thoughts and ideas.

What changes from Level 3 to Level 2 (see Figure 5.4)? At Level 2, the quality of the evidence is characterized as *inadequate* and *limited*. Descriptive indicators suggest that at a Level 2 scale point, the discourse climate may constrain

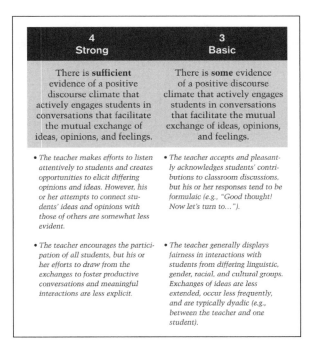

5 Exemplary	4 Strong
There is **compelling** evidence of a positive discourse climate that actively engages students in conversations that facilitate the mutual exchange of ideas, opinions, and feelings.	There is **sufficient** evidence of a positive discourse climate that actively engages students in conversations that facilitate the mutual exchange of ideas, opinions, and feelings.
• *The teacher deliberately fosters a climate in which expressing individual opinions and ideas is valued. He or she listens attentively to students and encourages them to listen and respond to one another.*	• *The teacher makes efforts to listen attentively to students and creates opportunities to elicit differing opinions and ideas. However, his or her attempts to connect students' ideas and opinions with those of others are somewhat less evident.*
• *The teacher explicitly and appropriately encourages the participation of all students, including those from differing linguistic, gender, racial, and cultural groups. The teacher skillfully builds on similarities and differences to foster productive conversation and meaningful interaction.*	• *The teacher encourages the participation of all students, but his or her efforts to draw from the exchanges to foster productive conversations and meaningful interactions are less explicit.*

Figure 5.2. Example of Level 5 and Level 4 descriptive indicators (bulleted items) for ELLCO K–3, Research Edition, Item 8, Discourse Climate.

4 Strong	3 Basic
There is **sufficient** evidence of a positive discourse climate that actively engages students in conversations that facilitate the mutual exchange of ideas, opinions, and feelings.	There is **some** evidence of a positive discourse climate that actively engages students in conversations that facilitate the mutual exchange of ideas, opinions, and feelings.
• *The teacher makes efforts to listen attentively to students and creates opportunities to elicit differing opinions and ideas. However, his or her attempts to connect students' ideas and opinions with those of others are somewhat less evident.*	• *The teacher accepts and pleasantly acknowledges students' contributions to classroom discussions, but his or her responses tend to be formulaic (e.g., "Good thought! Now let's turn to…").*
• *The teacher encourages the participation of all students, but his or her efforts to draw from the exchanges to foster productive conversations and meaningful interactions are less explicit.*	• *The teacher generally displays fairness in interactions with students from differing linguistic, gender, racial, and cultural groups. Exchanges of ideas are less extended, occur less frequently, and are typically dyadic (e.g., between the teacher and one student).*

Figure 5.3. Example of Level 4 and Level 3 descriptive indicators (bulleted items) for ELLCO K–3, Research Edition, Item 8, Discourse Climate.

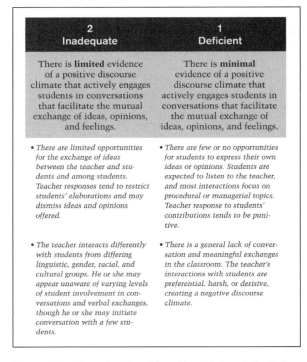

3 Basic	2 Inadequate
There is **some** evidence of a positive discourse climate that actively engages students in conversations that facilitate the mutual exchange of ideas, opinions, and feelings.	There is **limited** evidence of a positive discourse climate that actively engages students in conversations that facilitate the mutual exchange of ideas, opinions, and feelings.
• *The teacher accepts and pleasantly acknowledges students' contributions to classroom discussions, but his or her responses tend to be formulaic (e.g., "Good thought! Now let's turn to…").*	• *There are limited opportunities for the exchange of ideas between the teacher and students and among students. Teacher responses tend to restrict students' elaborations and may dismiss ideas and opinions offered.*
• *The teacher generally displays fairness in interactions with students from differing linguistic, gender, racial, and cultural groups. Exchanges of ideas are less extended, occur less frequently, and are typically dyadic (e.g., between the teacher and one student).*	• *The teacher interacts differently with students from differing linguistic, gender, racial, and cultural groups. He or she may appear unaware of varying levels of student involvement in conversations and verbal exchanges, though he or she may initiate conversation with a few students.*

Figure 5.4. Example of Level 3 and Level 2 descriptive indicators (bulleted items) for ELLCO K–3, Research Edition, Item 8, Discourse Climate.

2 Inadequate	1 Deficient
There is **limited** evidence of a positive discourse climate that actively engages students in conversations that facilitate the mutual exchange of ideas, opinions, and feelings.	There is **minimal** evidence of a positive discourse climate that actively engages students in conversations that facilitate the mutual exchange of ideas, opinions, and feelings.
• *There are limited opportunities for the exchange of ideas between the teacher and students and among students. Teacher responses tend to restrict students' elaborations and may dismiss ideas and opinions offered.*	• *There are few or no opportunities for students to express their own ideas or opinions. Students are expected to listen to the teacher, and most interactions focus on procedural or managerial topics. Teacher response to students' contributions tends to be punitive.*
• *The teacher interacts differently with students from differing linguistic, gender, racial, and cultural groups. He or she may appear unaware of varying levels of student involvement in conversations and verbal exchanges, though he or she may initiate conversation with a few students.*	• *There is a general lack of conversation and meaningful exchanges in the classroom. The teacher's interactions with students are preferential, harsh, or derisive, creating a negative discourse climate.*

Figure 5.5. Example of Level 2 and Level 1 descriptive indicators (bulleted items) for ELLCO K–3, Research Edition, Item 8, Discourse Climate.

students' interest and ability to participate actively and effectively in exchanges of ideas and information.

Again, the descriptive indicators change from Level 2 (*inadequate* and *limited*) to Level 1 (*deficient* and *minimal*) (see Figure 5.5). Level 1 is characterized by a negative discourse climate that severely restricts students' ability to participate and indicates patterns of unfair, unacceptable favoritism for some students.

FROM EVIDENCE TO RUBRIC TO RATING

In order to make a final score determination, the observer must consider the evidence taken in light of the rubric for each item.

Example 1: Item 8, Discourse Climate

Evidence for rating Item 8, Discourse Climate, is drawn from a teacher's ability to establish a positive and inclusive discourse climate that engages students in conversations and encourages them to exchange their ideas, opinions, and feelings. Figure 5.6 provides an excerpt of an observer's record of one of several conversations that took place in a kindergarten classroom when students were enjoying a midmorning snack. In Figure 5.6, below the filled-in page from the ELLCO K–3 is a recap of pertinent exchanges and events from the observation.

Although this is just a brief example, the observer's notes capture how the teacher fosters conversation in this kindergarten classroom. The teacher responds to Jayden (B2), by commenting, "I read the same thing." She later returns to Derek's point by stating, "But, you know, once a fire starts, those winds that Derek talked about can make it spread." In these and other ways, the teacher accepts and connects the students' different ideas—and is respectful of each student's contributions. She also seizes an opportunity to extend the students' understanding of the fires that have captured these students' attention by posing well-placed questions (e.g., "Can you tell us how, Jayden? What should people in California do to prevent these fires?"). Also important is the teacher's restraint in what she offers. She listens carefully to what the students' interests are concerning this topic and facilitates, rather than co-opting their informal, substantive exchange. Based on the strength of this example, in conjunction with other evidence seen throughout the observation, this classroom would receive a score of 5 for this item.

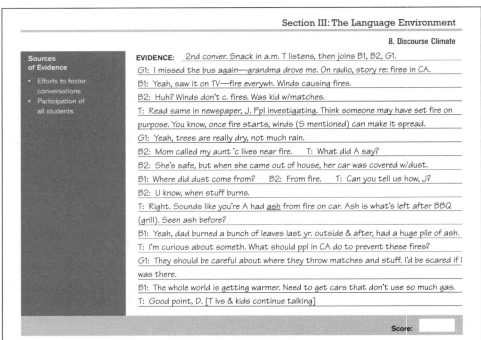

Sources of Evidence

• Efforts to foster conversations
• Participation of all students

EVIDENCE: 2nd conver. Snack in a.m. T listens, then joins B1, B2, G1.

G1: I missed the bus again—grandma drove me. On radio, story re: fires in CA.

B1: Yeah, saw it on TV—fire everywh. Winds causing fires.

B2: Huh? Winds don't c. fires. Was kid w/matches.

T: Read same in newspaper, J. Ppl investigating. Think someone may have set fire on purpose. You know, once fire starts, winds (S mentioned) can make it spread.

G1: Yeah, trees are really dry, not much rain.

B2: Mom called my aunt 'c lives near fire.   T: What did A say?

B2: She's safe, but when she came out of house, her car was covered w/dust.

B1: Where did dust come from?   B2: From fire.   T: Can you tell us how, J?

B2: U know, when stuff burns.

T: Right. Sounds like you're A had ash from fire on car. Ash is what's left after BBQ (grill). Seen ash before?

B1: Yeah, dad burned a bunch of leaves last yr. outside & after, had a huge pile of ash.

T: I'm curious about someth. What should ppl in CA do to prevent these fires?

G1: They should be careful about where they throw matches and stuff. I'd be scared if I was there.

B1: The whole world is getting warmer. Need to get cars that don't use so much gas.

T: Good point, D. [T lvs & kids continue talking]

Score:

Recap of Evidence

Three students are sitting together at a table during midmorning snack. The teacher joins the group when she overhears the conversation.

G1: I missed the bus again today, and my grandma had to drive me to school. On the radio there was a story about the huge fires in California.

B1: Yeah, I saw it on TV and the fire was everywhere. They said that these winds were causing the fire.

B2: Huh? Winds don't cause a fire. It was a kid with matches.

T: I was reading the newspaper and I read the same thing, Jayden. The people investigating the fires think that someone may have set the fire on purpose. But you know, once the fire starts, those winds that Derek talked about can make it spread.

G1: Yeah, and they said that the trees are really dry 'cause there's not much rain.

B2: My mom called my aunt 'cause she lives near the fires.

T: What did your aunt say?

B2: She's safe, but when she came out of her house, her car was covered with dust.

B1: Where did the dust come from?

B2: From the fire.

T: Can you tell us how, Jayden?

B2: You know when stuff burns.

T: Right. Sounds like your aunt had ash from the fire on her car. Ash is what is left after a fire, like at the bottom of a grill when you've had a barbecue. Have any of you seen ash before?

B1: Yeah, my dad burned a bunch of leaves last year outside and after, we had a huge pile of ash.

T: I'm curious about something. What should people in California do to prevent these fires?

G1: They should be really careful about where they throw matches and stuff. I'd be really scared if I was there!

B1: The whole world is getting warmer, you know, and we need to get cars that don't use so much gas.

T: That's a good point, Derek.

The teacher leaves, and the students continue talking.

Figure 5.6. Example of a completed evidence page (top) for ELLCO K–3, Research Edition, Item 8, Discourse Climate, and a recap of pertinent events from the observation session (bottom).

Sources of Evidence	EVIDENCE:
• Demonstration of cognitive strategies • Instructional strategies • Questioning to promote understanding	(15 min) Full grp. T in chair, kids on flr Ch. 8 of <u>My Father's Dragon</u> (Ruth Stiles Gannett) Introduces new chapter ("Elmer Meets a Gorilla"). Guess. After reading, goes back to a page w/sticky note on it. Reads sentence w/word <u>crossroads</u>. T: "If I didn't know what a crossroads was, I could use this picture that shows all the signs. Four different signs pointing in four different directions. The roads all meet here at the crossroads." (35 min) Small grp. <u>Fix-it</u> (David McPhail) 3 students (15 min) Before reading, shows title & author, picture on front. Make predictions & ask students to look for ways Emma's parents try to "fix it" (mark w/sticky notes). (15 min) During silent reading, students mark pages where parents tried to "fix it." (5 min) Very brief. T asks, "What was the most successful thing Emma's parents did to fix it?" (ran out of time)

Score: _____

Recap of Evidence

(15 minutes) Full-group read-aloud of Chapter 8 in *My Father's Dragon,* by Ruth Stiles Gannett. The teacher tells the group that today Elmer is going to meet another animal. She asks them to guess what animal it could be. She reads the chapter title "Elmer Meets a Gorilla," then reads the book, commenting on some of the pictures and interesting words. After reading, she goes back to a page with a sticky note on it. She rereads a sentence from the story that mentions the word *crossroads*. She goes on to explain, "Hmmm, if I was reading and I didn't know what a *crossroads* was, I could use the picture that shows all the signs. Four different signs pointing in four different directions. The roads all meet here at the crossroads."

(35 minutes) Small-group instruction with three students. Text: *Fix It!* by David McPhail

(15 minutes) Before reading the teacher introduces the book, then reads the title and author. She points to a picture on the cover and asks students to make predictions about what the story will be about. Entertains lots of predictions from the students. Then she sets a purpose for reading by asking the students to look for ways that Emma's parents try to "fix it." She asks them to mark this information with sticky notes.

(15 minutes) During silent reading, students mark pages where Emma's parents tried to "fix it."

(5 minutes) This discussion was brief. After reading, teacher asks, "What do you think was the most successful thing Emma's parents did to fix it?" "What evidence is there that it was successful?"

Figure 5.7. Example of a completed evidence page (top) for ELLCO K–3, Research Edition, Item 15, Strategies to Build Reading Comprehension, and a recap of pertinent events from the observation session (bottom).

Example 2: Item 15, Strategies to Build Reading Comprehension

Evidence for Item 15, Strategies to Build Reading Comprehension, includes demonstration of cognitive strategies, observation of instructional strategies, and questioning to promote understanding. Figure 5.7 on the previous page shows a sample evidence page from a completed observation form for Item 15.

In this second-grade example, the teacher begins the reading block with a full-group read-aloud of Chapter 8 in *My Father's Dragon*, by Ruth Stiles Gannett. After reading the book, the teacher explains and demonstrates the cognitive strategy of using context clues to define and explore the meaning of *crossroads*. The teacher then makes the transition to a small-group instructional session using *Fix-it*, by David McPhail. Before reading, the teacher sets a purpose for reading in terms of looking for ways the parents of the main character,

Figure 5.8. Example of Level 5 and Level 4 descriptive indicators (bulleted items) for ELLCO K–3, Research Edition, Item 15, Strategies to Build Reading Comprehension.

Emma, try to "fix it" (their television is broken). As the students read silently, they use sticky notes to make a record of noted evidence. After the reading, the teacher poses a question about the most effective way to "fix it."

In order to rate this item or any other, observers should begin at Level 5. Because of the strength of the evidence noted for this item, the rating decision requires considering a Level 5 versus a Level 4. This was a strong, engaging level of instruction that moved beyond a basic level (see Figure 5.8). Reaching a decision requires balancing the specific evidence in relation to the descriptive indicators and referring back to the anchor statements of the rubric. In this case, a preponderance of the evidence falls within Level 4. The teacher points to an illustration in the book and tells the students that she knows what a *crossroads* is from the picture and that the students can use pictures to help understand a word's meaning. Her explanation, however, does not provide alternative strategies for using context clues, particularly when a picture is not available. The small-group lesson uses an integrated set of instructional strategies before, during, and after reading, but the amount of time devoted before reading substantially diminished the amount of time available for the after-reading discussion.

Example 3: Item 16, Writing Environment

Evidence for Item 16, Writing Environment, is derived from observations of the teacher creating varied opportunities to motivate students to write. Furthermore, this item considers the ways in which the teacher organizes and offers feedback as well as the quality of the displays of the students' and the teacher's writing. A sample page with notes taken for Item 16 is shown in Figure 5.9.

In this example from a third-grade classroom, the observer notes examples of the way the teacher interacts with students around writing. She engages with individual students in a series of conferences in which she briefly talks to the students about the ideas in their piece and then critiques their work. Other students, not conferring with the teacher, are writing a "Just So" story (in the manner of Rudyard Kipling's *Just So Stories*). Examples of students' writing posted around the room reside on a bulletin board titled November Book Reports.

In this case, initial review of the evidence would lead an observer to consider Level 4, Level 3, and Level 2 anchor statements and descriptive indicators (see Figure 5.10). The evidence is clearly not *compelling*, so Level 5 is not considered. There might be, however, *sufficient*, *some*, or *limited* evidence, depending on the specific characteristics of the interactions and classroom displays noted. Once again, the trained observer must analyze the rubric at each level and consider the evidence. The teacher is providing time to confer with

Section V: Print and Writing

16. Writing Environment

Sources of Evidence

- Varied opportunities
- Teacher role
- Feedback
- Content of displays

EVIDENCE: Writer's Workshop
T conferences w/5 students individually. Asks each student the same ques.: what they like most about the "Just So" story. She points out strong & weak vbs in their stories. Suggests alternatives strengthening weak vbs. Other students are writing—engaged. T reminds them that the story they're writing must use an animal and explain a physical characteristic. Only student work displayed on bulletin board—"November Book Reports."

Score:

Recap of Evidence

Writer's Workshop (1 hour)

The teacher holds conferences with five students individually. She asks each the same question: "What do you like most about your 'Just So' story?" She points out "strong" and "weak" verbs and suggests alternatives. Other students are writing–engaged. The teacher reminds them that their stories must use a real animal and explain a physical characteristic. The only student work displayed is tacked to a bulletin board labeled "November Book Reports."

Figure 5.9. Example of a completed evidence page (top) for ELLCO K–3, Research Edition, Item 16, Writing Environment, and a recap of pertinent events from the observation session (bottom).

individual students and there is some attention to the ideas in the piece, which distinguishes the evidence from the Level 2 category. The "Just So" story activity that the students are currently working on conforms to a prescribed format that restricts students' opportunities to express themselves more authentically. Also the book report display distinguishes the evidence from the Level 4 category. In sum, the evidence leads to a score determination of 3 (*basic*).

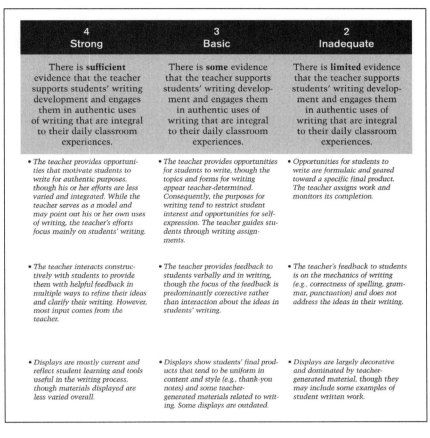

4 Strong	3 Basic	2 Inadequate
There is **sufficient** evidence that the teacher supports students' writing development and engages them in authentic uses of writing that are integral to their daily classroom experiences.	There is **some** evidence that the teacher supports students' writing development and engages them in authentic uses of writing that are integral to their daily classroom experiences.	There is **limited** evidence that the teacher supports students' writing development and engages them in authentic uses of writing that are integral to their daily classroom experiences.
• *The teacher provides opportunities that motivate students to write for authentic purposes, though his or her efforts are less varied and integrated. While the teacher serves as a model and may point out his or her own uses of writing, the teacher's efforts focus mainly on students' writing.*	• *The teacher provides opportunities for students to write, though the topics and forms for writing appear teacher-determined. Consequently, the purposes for writing tend to restrict student interest and opportunities for self-expression. The teacher guides students through writing assignments.*	• *Opportunities for students to write are formulaic and geared toward a specific final product. The teacher assigns work and monitors its completion.*
• *The teacher interacts constructively with students to provide them with helpful feedback in multiple ways to refine their ideas and clarify their writing. However, most input comes from the teacher.*	• *The teacher provides feedback to students verbally and in writing, though the focus of the feedback is predominantly corrective rather than interaction about the ideas in students' writing.*	• *The teacher's feedback to students is on the mechanics of writing (e.g., correctness of spelling, grammar, punctuation) and does not address the ideas in their writing.*
• *Displays are mostly current and reflect student learning and tools useful in the writing process, though materials displayed are less varied overall.*	• *Displays show students' final products that tend to be uniform in content and style (e.g., thank-you notes) and some teacher-generated materials related to writing. Some displays are outdated.*	• *Displays are largely decorative and dominated by teacher-generated material, though they may include some examples of student written work.*

Figure 5.10. Example of Levels 4, 3, and 2 descriptive indicators (bulleted items) for ELLCO K–3, Research Edition, Item 16, Writing Environment.

6

Using the ELLCO K–3 for Professional Development

The ELLCO K–3 offers practitioners a vision for evidence-based practices that support students' language and literacy development in the primary grades. The structure of the instrument is explicitly designed—through the use of carefully crafted descriptive indicators—to provide a continuum that can help teachers see where they are now and where they want to go. Accordingly, the ELLCO K–3 can be used as an effective professional development tool to help teachers build their understanding of the essential features of language and literacy learning that will enhance their own classrooms.

Schools and districts engage in many types of professional development activities. Those that are carried out over time, employ multiple support strategies, and engage teachers as active participants in the planning and assessment have been found to lead to more sustained, positive changes (Dickinson & Brady, 2006; Landry, Swank, Smith, & Assel, 2006). Whatever your staff development design may be, the ELLCO K–3 can supplement your efforts in multiple ways. For instance, many schools are using literacy coaches to improve reading proficiency. In such cases, the tool can be used to make initial assessments and track changes over time. The ELLCO K–3 offers a common set of practices that teachers and coaches together can use to note progress and identify areas that require more attention.

Other schools are adopting a study-group approach as an alternative to more traditional workshops. In such settings, teachers gather regularly to explore a common issue relevant to their practice, sometimes orchestrated by a specialist from the district. The ELLCO K–3 can serve as a basis for organizing such professional conversations when the topic is literacy. By using various sections of the tool (e.g., Section IV: Books and Reading) as a springboard for discussion and the exchange of ideas, the ELLCO K–3 can be a practical aid in

47

teacher development. In the following sections, we suggest specific ideas about how to incorporate the ELLCO K–3 into efforts to strengthen the quality of language and literacy practices in kindergarten through third-grade classrooms.

TIPS FOR INCORPORATING THE ELLCO K–3 INTO LANGUAGE AND LITERACY PRACTICES

Step 1: Create a Positive Climate for Teacher Development

Your work as a professional development leader or supervisor is parallel to that of teachers. Just as teachers seek to create positive, stimulating learning environments for students, so also do supervisors and others concerned with teacher development. Teachers have become increasingly sensitive to assessment instruments as a means of monitoring their compliance and performance. Therefore, from the start it is vital to introduce the ELLCO K–3 as a way to stimulate thinking about practice rather than as a summative appraisal of performance. To create a safe environment for teachers' reflection and motivation to learn, consider the following suggestions:

- Begin by engaging in a discussion with teachers about their own goals for growth and learning. Ask them what they hope to learn, and probe for areas of strength and accomplishment.

- Clarify the role you expect to play in the professional development and your partnership in the learning process. If you are supervising the teachers you are working with, underscore how your role in professional development is distinct from your regular oversight.

- Emphasize that the process inherent in becoming a reflective practitioner is at its core developmental in nature. Stress that change happens over time— for teachers as well as students.

- Keep the focus on student learning and engagement. Describe ways that the ELLCO K–3 can be used to understand complex features of the classroom that influence language and literacy development.

- Make your own intentions transparent. Articulate your goals for using the ELLCO K–3 in the professional development process by describing why you have selected it and how you will use it. Reinforce the ways that teachers are integral to the process and encourage them to become critical observers of their own practices.

Step 2: Preview the ELLCO K–3 Together

Both the tool itself and the *ELLCO K–3 User's Guide* contain a wealth of relevant information that can help teachers develop a vision of exemplary practices and understand the research base. The guide also presents many teacher-friendly resources that can be used in a range of creative ways. What is important is that you encourage teachers to view the materials directly but discuss them together. Some ways to begin your collaborative review include

- Articulate your goals for using the ELLCO K–3 in this process, describing why you have selected it and how you will use it. Reinforce that teachers' engagement is essential because an important determinant of success is teachers' ability to become critical assessors of their own practices.

- Read and discuss Chapter 2, "Effective Elements of Early Literacy: Kenny's Story," which provides vignettes that describe how a student's experiences in first grade can enrich language and literacy learning. Consider posing questions after each vignette to provoke thinking about Mrs. Porter's role in bringing about Kenny's actions and reactions. Discuss the implications of each vignette for practice. Highlight those areas that are tied to teachers' own goals for professional development.

- Use Kenny's Story as a deliberate vehicle for becoming familiar with the ELLCO K–3. Initially, the rubrics for rating items (Levels 5 through 1) that are used in the tool can be overwhelming to some primary-grade teachers who may be unaccustomed to using such guides to assess student work; this strategy is more common in upper elementary grades and beyond. Appearing after each vignette in Kenny's Story is a list of ELLCO K–3 items that could be rated in part when considering each snapshot of teaching and learning. Introducing the items and the rubric in such a measured way may make the tool more accessible to many teachers.

- Review the range of resources listed at the end of the book, including a comprehensive list of web sites, web-based resources, books, and articles germane to early language and literacy classroom practices. Selected for their relevance at different levels of sophistication, these materials can provide teachers with information about evidence-based practices as well as concrete assistance such as selecting books for their classroom. Take time to identify specific resources that map on to teachers' professional goals and bring them to their attention.

- Read and discuss examples of items and ratings from this user's guide. If the whole tool seems overwhelming at first, settle on one or two of the five sections for an initial focus. Help teachers decode the rubric for rating each item. One way to get teachers accustomed to the rubric language is to have them highlight the areas that are different for each descriptive indicator, moving from Level 5 (*exemplary*) across the scale to Level 1 (*deficient*), in the same manner observers would to prepare for an observation.

Step 3: Conduct an Initial Observation

The ELLCO K–3 can be used flexibly for professional development purposes. For example, you might choose to complete just one section per observation or focus on a limited number of items that are most important to a particular teacher or classroom. Observing in classrooms can be rewarding and challenging. Follow the guidelines for observation in Chapter 4, "How to Conduct an ELLCO K–3 Observation," to ensure that you are as fair and impartial as possible.

• Be sure to set up a mutually agreeable time for an initial observation. Consider the teacher's goals and select a time and a day when the teacher will be engaged in instruction that is likely to provide fruitful material for a post-observation debriefing. Also arrange a time when you can meet to discuss the observation. It is usually difficult to debrief immediately after the observation, but it is critical to discuss it soon—preferably on the same day—otherwise the events will lose their freshness, especially for the teacher.

• Take plenty of notes that will serve as evidence of what you see and hear during your observation. Evidence not only helps you decide on a rating, it also provides the concrete examples that will form the basis of your post-observation conversation with the teacher. The more detailed and specific the notes, the more effective you can be in providing thoughtful feedback.

• Maintain an unobtrusive presence in the classroom while observing. Pay particular attention to preserving a neutral expression, despite what you might see or hear. Teachers will be anxious to get your quick, "sound bite" feedback before you leave, so be prepared. You might simply say, "Thanks for letting me observe. I enjoyed it and appreciated observing your writing conferences. I'll see you at the end of the day."

• Many coaches use videotape as a tool in professional development. To ensure a stable picture with good-quality sound, it is important to use a tripod and a microphone that will pick up what the teacher and students say. It is most effective if you focus your taping on a particular activity, for instance, small-group literature circles. View the videotaped footage with the teacher; it will serve as an effective springboard for debriefing with the teacher.

Step 4: Share Results

For many literacy coaches and supervisors, sharing the results of an ELLCO K–3 observation can be intimidating. Here are some strategies for structuring feedback conversations in ways that are positive and supportive and that lead toward productive goal setting.

- Remind the teacher that this initial observation is to be used as the basis for a beginning conversation about what is currently happening in the classroom and to generate goals for changing and improving practices.

- Remind yourself and the teacher of the big picture you are both working toward, to provide opportunities and experiences for students that support their learning in multiple areas of development, with particular consideration given to language and literacy learning.

- Ask the teacher for his or her perspective first. Be prepared to probe and wait if the teacher feels reluctant. Many teachers equate their reflection on what happened to criticism. Some, therefore, only discuss what was problematic. Others, who may be reticent to indicate that they were pleased with the outcome, may say nothing at all. You can assist teachers unaccustomed to reflecting on practice by modeling an approach. In the face of silence, you can *briefly* recap an event observed, probing for a teacher's assessment. What is essential is that the teacher, not you, be the main contributor to the conversation. Avoid filling the silence with your own assessment.

- If you are videotaping your observation, find a time to review the videotape before meeting with the teacher, noting your questions and feedback. At the debriefing, view the footage with the teacher, making sure you use the aforementioned strategies to elicit the teacher's reactions first.

- As much as possible, link your own feedback to the teacher's comments. Begin by sharing some positive points from your observation, then move into reviewing specific items and ratings. Remember to emphasize strengths and couple comments about weaknesses with suggestions for alternative approaches.

Step 5: Generate Goals

Based on one or more observations and debriefings, you should have a good baseline understanding of the starting point and even preliminary goals for professional development. Setting goals is an iterative process; as you and the teachers become more comfortable in this mentoring relationship, goals will be refined and expanded. When setting goals,

- Begin with some concrete areas that are more easily influenced, such as a focus on the selection and organization of books. Move steadily toward ideas that require more substantive change, such as the curriculum and instructional approach (e.g., how books are used to support content learning).

- Use the ELLCO K–3 descriptive indicators as a way to prompt teachers to articulate their own criteria for success. At the same time that you are building teachers' knowledge and skill in early literacy, you also are promoting the development of reflective practitioners.

- Establish a reasonable timeframe for change. Some teachers tend to be overly ambitious about how quickly they can adopt new practices and consequently get discouraged when it takes longer than originally anticipated. Inject some realism and analysis to balance the initial enthusiasm that you may encounter. Remind teachers that concrete environmental changes are easier to implement than those that require modifications in interaction and instruction.

BEGINNING STEPS TOWARD CHANGE

The overall goal of professional development is to build a cadre of reflective practitioners who are intentional in what they teach and how they teach it. Such teachers are constantly engaged in refining their skills and assessing their own effectiveness in light of student learning. The ELLCO K–3 can play a significant role in transforming practice, but it will be most effective if used as a part of an ongoing, coherent system of quality improvement and professional development. The ideas presented next are offered to help supervisors, literacy coaches, and others tie their support activities to the five sections of the ELLCO K–3.

Section I: Classroom Structure
(Organization, Contents, Management, Professional Focus)

Beginning with an analysis of the physical environment is typically a comfortable, concrete way for teachers to begin to reflect on the what, why, and how of their classrooms. Some ways to encourage analysis might include

- Mapping the layout of the classroom (What considerations go into an effective classroom layout?)

- Observing and mapping patterns of traffic flow (How do students and teachers actually use the space? Are there areas of congestion? Do unused areas exist?)

- Listing classroom areas and their intended uses

- Conducting an inventory of materials in the classroom

- Observing and recording students' actual use of classroom areas

- Tracking time spent in management activities and conversations

- Tracking time spent in transitions

Section II: Curriculum
(Integration of Language and Literacy, Independence, Diversity)

Facilitating students' development and learning through curriculum includes many facets, and the curriculum section of the ELLCO K–3 delineates several areas for consideration. Integrating language and literacy across the curriculum, encouraging student independence in learning, and attending to the diverse needs of individual learners within the context of daily classroom life are challenges for most teachers. Here are some ways to begin thinking about these intertwined strands:

- Look critically at patterns of time use, scheduling, and grouping in the classroom, analyzing the amount and quality of time spent in varied settings, groupings, and activities connected to learning.

- Look for ways that specific language and literacy activities can be infused into the content-area curriculum. List curriculum topics and themes, describing general and specific learning goals and activities that relate to those goals, weaving in language and literacy as appropriate.

- Observe, note, and analyze areas of diversity among classroom members; in addition to more obvious characteristics, this might also include considering diverse approaches to learning (e.g., Jacob learns best when he can use his entire body; Lucy prefers to observe before joining).

- Brainstorm approaches to curriculum planning that capitalize on the diversity of the group and the strengths and needs of individuals, then try out curriculum plans and ideas, assessing strengths and areas for improvement.

Section III: The Language Environment (Discourse Climate, Extended Conversations, Vocabulary)

The items in this section of the ELLCO K–3 are derived from extensive research that has pinpointed specific characteristics of talk that build students' language skills. For many teachers, becoming aware of their own language use with students is, in itself, an eye-opening experience that leads to reflective analysis and reconsideration of their tone, conversational topics, and use of vocabulary. Here are some ways to begin this process:

- Tape record interactions in the classroom and analyze them for substance and turn taking.

- Brainstorm familiar and new topics and associated challenging vocabulary (e.g., concept webbing, KWL [What I Know, What I Want to Know, What I Have Learned], research).

- Generate initial questions, comments, or activities that might provoke students' interest in a topic, along with ideas for introducing vocabulary.

Section IV: Books and Reading (Characteristics, Sounds to Print, Fluency, Vocabulary, Comprehension)

The book-related items on the ELLCO K–3 delineate a variety of ways in which books can be used to facilitate and extend learning, as well as criteria to be considered when teaching students to read. Next are some ways to begin thinking about books and reading:

- Conduct an inventory of books and an analysis of their characteristics along varied dimensions (e.g., condition, difficulty of text, range of topics, quality of illustrations, diversity of genres and characters).

- Seek out, read aloud, and supply the classroom with a wide range of high-quality books at varying levels of difficulty. List classroom interest areas and generate ideas for how books might be meaningfully incorporated within them.

- Explore together with teachers instructional strategies that support students' reading fluency, including choral reading, repeated readings, readers' theater (adapting a story for performance), and opportunities for students to read aloud. Be available to support teachers' efforts to employ new instructional techniques.

- Critically evaluate the place and prominence of phonics instruction in the context of the overall reading program. Research or brainstorm alternative methods to meet goals for fostering phonemic awareness (e.g., sound games, visual/verbal cuing), and encourage the trying of new strategies.

- Preread books to prepare for book reading with students, generate questions and comments in advance of reading, select specific vocabulary to focus on, and plan for curriculum extensions related to books and words selected. Plan discussions and activities for students that focus their attention on word meanings and ways to use context to derive plausible meanings during reading.

- Expose teachers to challenging texts and have them analyze their own approaches to decoding, accessing word meanings, and comprehending what they are reading. Placing teachers in the same position as their students can support their understanding of the difficulties students often encounter during reading.

Section V: Print and Writing (Environment, Instruction, Student Writing)

Students who are surrounded by multiple and diverse examples of spoken and written language develop a rich understanding of how words work and how print and words are connected. The items of the ELLCO K–3 that are focused on writing delineate several ways that teachers can structure the classroom environment and their interactions with students to facilitate and support the emerging capacities of their students as readers and writers. Some additional suggestions for looking in detail at writing opportunities in the classroom follow:

- Analyze the current procedure for tracking student writing and providing feedback to students. What processes are in use? Are there additional strategies, structures, or approaches that could deepen students' understanding of the purposes and process of writing?

- Collect and display samples of students' writing, seeking to understand the purposes of their writing and what messages they are trying to communicate.

- Assess the functional daily uses of writing in the classroom for teachers (e.g., morning message) and students (e.g., use of a sign-in routine) to build on and expand the ways writing is used.

- Explore teachers' role in modeling and supporting students' writing (e.g., what motivations, prompts, and strategies for feedback seem most useful for students?)

- List, discuss, and analyze existing environmental print, brainstorming additional strategies for the inclusion of meaningful environmental print in the classroom.

REFERENCES

Dickinson, D.K., & Brady, J.P. (2006). Toward effective support for language and literacy through professional development. In M. Zaslow & I. Martinez-Beck (Eds.), *Critical issues in early childhood professional development* (pp. 141–170). Baltimore: Paul H. Brookes Publishing Co..

Landry, S.H., Swank, P.R., Smith, K.E., & Assel, M.A. (2006). Enhancing early literacy skills for preschool children: Bringing a professional development model to scale. *Journal of Learning Disabilities, 39*(4), 306–324.

Using the
ELLCO K–3 in Research

Using the ELLCO K–3 for research requires skilled observers in order to maintain high standards of accuracy. Observers selected to collect data should be familiar with primary grades, have knowledge of early reading and writing, and have classroom observation experience. Even when observers meet all of these criteria, individuals may approach their observations differently because of their unique perspectives and experiences. Two individuals with similar training can view the same phenomenon differently, so there is the potential for measurement error in any observational rating scale. Steps that can be taken to reduce measurement error include training, practicing and calibrating ratings, calculating interrater reliability, and recalibrating ratings while collecting data.

TRAINING

ELLCO K–3 training provides observers with a common lens through which to view classrooms while conducting their observations. ELLCO K–3 training consists of a careful review of all of the items and focuses on the evidence associated with each item. Training provides participants with an opportunity to observe and score actual classrooms in order to become familiar with recording evidence and choosing the appropriate rating. Each opportunity to rate an item should be followed by a conversation with trainers to compare ratings, discuss appropriate scores, and review areas of disagreement. As a result, data collectors leave the training session with a common idea of how to approach observations and assign scores.

PRACTICING AND CALIBRATING RATINGS

In addition to traditional user training, data collectors should practice using the ELLCO K–3 in several classrooms prior to conducting any observations that will serve as a data point. Conduct these practice sessions in teams or small groups and follow each observation with a debriefing conversation to calibrate ratings. Observers should compare ratings and discuss their rationale for assigning each score based on the evidence noted to support their judgments. These conversations are vital exercises that enable observation teams to come to consensus on difficult scoring decisions. The nature and extent of the evidence recorded are useful ways to gauge an individual's ability to both harvest and represent relevant information during classroom observations. Relying on memory will be problematic, especially when data collectors work across numerous classrooms in a compressed timeframe.

INTERRATER RELIABILITY

In order to be confident that individuals are rating classrooms reliably, observers should conduct joint observations to calculate interrater reliability, or the degree of agreement among raters. Options for calculation of interrater reliability include a simple calculation of the percentage of agreement (the number of items given identical ratings divided by the total number of items) as well as more robust estimates that take into account agreement that might occur by chance such as Cohen's kappa (Cohen, 1960; used when there are two raters) and Fleiss's kappa (Fleiss, 1981; used when there are more than two raters). Landis and Koch (1977) indicated that a kappa of .40–.59 is moderate interrater reliability, a kappa of .60–.79 is substantial, and a kappa of .80 is outstanding. A kappa estimate of .70, however, is generally considered acceptable interrater reliability (Subkoviak, 1988). It is up to the researcher to decide which estimate and level of interrater reliability is appropriate for his or her research study.

RECALIBRATION IN THE FIELD

In most research and evaluation activities, there is substantial time pressure to gather pre- and postintervention data. Once the training of data collectors is complete, often observers are scheduled to visit multiple classrooms in the field, cycling completed forms back to the research team. If observers are left on their own, their ratings can drift over time. Some may become overconfident of their understanding of the rubric and lax about taking evidence and using it against the rubric to settle on a rating. Others may slowly drift to their own heuristic and begin scoring items based on their own rubric, affecting the reliability of the ratings. It is, therefore, advisable to recalibrate data collectors' ratings to ensure that they are using the tool correctly. Recalibration with an expert observer should occur approximately at the midpoint of the data collection schedule. Some would advise that it should take place within 2 weeks of the original training. The recalibration process involves scheduling a joint observation (i.e., both the expert observer and data collector) and debriefing afterward using the same protocols that were put in place during the initial training.

REFERENCES

Cohen, J. (1960). A coefficient of agreement for nominal scales. *Educational and Psychological Measurement, 20,* 37–46.

Fleiss, J.L. (1981). *Statistical methods for rates and proportions* (2nd ed.). New York: John Wiley & Sons.

Landis, J.R., & Koch, G. (1977). The measurement of observer agreement for categorical data. *Biometrics, 33,* 159–174.

Subkoviak, M.J. (1988, Spring). A practitioner's guide to computation and interpretation of reliability indices for mastery tests. *Journal of Educational Measurement, 25*(1), 47–55.

Technical Report on the ELLCO Toolkit, Research Edition

Note for the Reader

As described in Chapter 1, the original ELLCO Toolkit, Research Edition (Smith & Dickinson, 2002a), has been reworked into a suite of observation instruments. What initially served to guide observations of pre-K and K–3 classrooms is now represented by two distinct instruments: the ELLCO Pre-K (Smith, Brady, & Anastasopoulos, 2008) and the ELLCO K–3, Research Edition. Thanks to the widespread use of the original toolkit, feedback from the field, and the examination of current research on reading and writing, we have created the ELLCO K–3, Research Edition, as a new instrument. Therefore, specific psychometric analyses of the current ELLCO K–3 will be reported as the tool is used in current and planned research. These include interrater reliability; general descriptive statistics; measures of internal consistency and validity, stability, and change; correlations with other established measures; and predictive validity. The data presented in the following report may provide a useful reference for those interested in the technical qualities of the original toolkit.

This technical report provides data that were collected from 1997 to 2002 as part of the development of the ELLCO Toolkit, Research Edition, as well as additional data that were collected from 2002 to 2007 using the published toolkit. The ELLCO Toolkit, Research Edition, was pilot tested and used in several research studies from its development, with the minor revisions that typically occur through practical use and feedback, through its original publication in

2002. This included research conducted in more than 150 preschool classrooms for the Head Start–funded New England Quality Research Center (NEQRC) (funder: U.S. Department of Health and Human Services, Administration for Children and Families; 1995–2000) and the Literacy Environment Enrichment Program (LEEP) (funder: U.S. Department of Education, Office of Educational Research and Improvement; 2000–2003), both based in the Center for Children & Families (CC&F) at Education Development Center, Inc., in Newton, Massachusetts. Since its initial publication, researchers at CC&F have used the ELLCO Toolkit, Research Edition, in more than 250 classrooms as part of six different projects:

- The New England Quality Research Center: The Next Generation (funder: U.S. Department of Health and Human Services, Administration for Children and Families; 2001–2006)

- Examining the Efficacy of Two Models of Preschool Professional Development in Language and Literacy (funder: U.S. Department of Education, Institute of Education Sciences; 2005–2007)

- Child Care Quality: Does Partnership Make a Difference—an Extension of the Partnership Impact Project (funder: U.S. Department of Education, 2004–2007)

- Evaluation of the Newport Early Reading First Collaborative (funder: U.S. Department of Education, 2003–2006)

- Evaluation of the Springfield Early Reading First Initiative (funder: U.S. Department of Education, 2003–2007)

- Connecticut Is Reading First (funder: U.S. Department of Education, 2005 to present)

All of these projects are concerned with the language and literacy development of children from lower income families and communities. Because of this, data reported here are based on centers and classrooms in lower income communities.

The data reported in the main body of this technical report come from 30 classrooms from the NEQRC study and a total of 117 classrooms for the LEEP study. Each of the NEQRC classrooms was observed on one occasion, whereas most of the LEEP classrooms were observed on two occasions (fall and spring), and a few LEEP classrooms were visited a total of three times. In the data used to calculate means, correlations, and Cronbach's alpha, each visit to a classroom is counted as a separate observation. In the data used to report stability and change (LEEP classrooms only), each LEEP classroom is counted only once, and fall and spring scores are treated as distinct variables.

An addendum to the original research at the end of this technical report describes Cronbach's alpha analyses performed using a larger sample of data collected between 2002 and 2007. These data are from a total of 259 classrooms from the following projects:

- The New England Quality Research Center: The Next Generation ($n = 57$)

- Examining the Efficacy of Two Models of Preschool Professional Development in Language and Literacy ($n = 67$)

- Child Care Quality: Does Partnership Make a Difference—an Extension of the Partnership Impact Project ($n = 66$)

- Evaluation of the Newport Early Reading First Collaborative ($n = 26$)

- Evaluation of the Springfield Early Reading First Initiative ($n = 22$)

- Connecticut Is Reading First ($n = 21$)

As with the data used for the Cronbach's alpha analyses initially reported in the technical appendix of the *User's Guide to the Early Language and Literacy Classroom Observation Toolkit, Research Edition* (Smith & Dickinson, 2002b), some classrooms were visited on multiple occasions, and each classroom visit was counted as a separate observation.

PSYCHOMETRIC PROPERTIES OF THE LITERACY ENVIRONMENT CHECKLIST

The psychometric properties presented for the Literacy Environment Checklist (ELLCO Toolkit, Research Edition) are based on data from Year 4 of the NEQRC project combined with data from Years 1–3 of the LEEP project. Data from the NEQRC project were collected during the winter of 1998–1999 ($n = 29$). The data from Year 1 of the LEEP project were collected in the fall of 1998 ($n = 26$) and the spring of 1999 ($n = 26$). Data from Year 2 of the LEEP project were collected in the fall of 1999 ($n = 42$) and spring of 2000 ($n = 38$). Data from Year 3 of the LEEP project were collected in the fall of 2000 ($n = 47$) and spring of 2001 ($n = 47$). Together, the projects resulted in a total sample size of 255, although the actual subsample sizes vary depending on the analyses conducted. Many of the classrooms included were in Head Start programs. Unlike the Classroom Observation, the Literacy Environment Checklist and the Literacy Activities Rating Scale have been used for research only in preschool classrooms and were designed specifically to help identify the impact of our literacy intervention in those classrooms. They have not been used to predict students' growth; rather, they have been used in conjunction with the Classroom Observation to pinpoint the specific effects of a literacy intervention.

The items from the Literacy Environment Checklist of the ELLCO Toolkit, Research Edition, have been incorporated in the main body of the ELLCO Pre-K and have informed the development of new items in the ELLCO K–3. The Literacy Environment Checklist is not included in the ELLCO Pre-K or K–3.

Interrater Reliability

Research use of the Literacy Environment Checklist was predicated on the appropriate training of observers. We have required that prospective observers be familiar with theories of early literacy development and have an understanding of the range of instructional methods that are typically used in classrooms. Prospective observers received a daylong training session on using the ELLCO Toolkit, Research Edition, which included background information on language and literacy development, explanation of the toolkit, and videotape examples; then training session participants received a second day of supervised practice in using the toolkit. When observers were trained and supervised appropriately, we achieved an average interrater reliability of 88% with relative ease. (This interrater reliability rate is for agreements within 1 point of each other on the rating scale.)

General Statistics

On the basis of our theoretical beliefs and preliminary analysis of the data, we created three summary variables for the Literacy Environment Checklist: the *Books* subtotal, the *Writing* subtotal, and the *Total* score. The *Books* subtotal includes all items from the Book Area, Book Selection, and Book Use sections of the checklist. The *Writing* subtotal includes all items from the Writing Materials and Writing Around the Room sections. Table A.1 reports descriptive sta-

Table A.1. Descriptive statistics for subscale and total score data for the Literacy Environment Checklist in the ELLCO Toolkit, Research Edition ($n = 255$)

Composite variable	Mean	Standard deviation	Minimum	Maximum
Books subscale	11.13	3.90	2.00	20.00
Writing subscale	10.44	4.22	1.00	20.00
Literacy Environment Checklist Total score	21.57	7.37	5.00	40.00

Table A.2. Cronbach's alpha for data for the Literacy Environment Checklist in the ELLCO Toolkit, Research Edition ($n = 255$)

Composite variable	Alpha
Books subtotal	.73
Writing subtotal	.75
Literacy Environment Checklist Total score	.84

tistics for Literacy Environment Checklist data gathered as part of the NEQRC and LEEP studies ($n = 255$).

Reliability Analysis

Reliability analysis was conducted to examine the internal consistency of the Literacy Environment Checklist. Table A.2 shows the alphas obtained for the *Total* score as well as for the two subtotals. Cronbach's alpha of .84 for the *Total* score shows good internal consistency. All item–total correlations were moderate to high ($r = .54$ to $r = .55$).

Cronbach's alpha of .73 for the *Books* subtotal shows good internal consistency for this composite. All item–total correlations were moderate ($r = .21$ to $r = .54$) with the exception of Item 1 in the Book Area section ("Is an area set aside just for book reading?"), which exhibited a correlation of .16.

Cronbach's alpha for the *Writing* subtotal was .75, also indicating somewhat low but still acceptable internal consistency. Item–total correlations ranged from a low of .21 for Item 15 in the Writing Materials section ("Are there templates or tools to help children form letters?") to a high of .59 for Item 21 in the Writing Around the Room section ("How many varieties of children's writing are on display in the classroom?").

Measuring Stability and Change

Using the data collected from the LEEP classrooms, we reported preliminary findings on the ability of the Literacy Environment Checklist to measure both stability and change over time (see Table A.3). When one looks at mean scores across the 3 years of the LEEP project, the fall scores of the intervention are slightly higher on the three dimensions of the Literacy Environment Checklist than the comparison group. (For the fall scores in the LEEP study, differences between the intervention group and comparison group on the Literacy Environment Checklist were statistically significant for the *Writing* subtotal only; $t = -2.62$, $p < .05$). In the spring, the comparison group showed significant change

Table A.3.   Stability and change in Literacy Environment Checklist scores (ELLCO Toolkit, Research Edition), fall and spring means, for Years 1–3 of the Literacy Environment Enrichment Program (LEEP)

	Fall		Spring	
Composite variable	Comparison group ($n = 38$)	LEEP intervention ($n = 40$)	Comparison group ($n = 38$)	LEEP intervention ($n = 40$)
Books subtotal	9.25	10.53	10.45 ($t = 3.27, p < .01$)	14.84 ($t = 7.18, p < .001$)
Writing subtotal	8.77	11.21	9.12 ($t = 1.14, p = $ n.s.)	14.26 ($t = 5.72, p < .001$)
Literacy Environment Checklist *Total* score	18.12	20.86	19.52 ($t = 2.87, p < .01$)	29.03 ($t = 7.82, p < .001$)

n.s., not significant.

on the *Total* score as well as on the *Books* subtotal yet remained stable on the *Writing* subtotal. As hoped, the intervention group scores changed significantly from fall to spring in all categories. These changes resulted in intervention group scores that were statistically significantly different from the comparison group scores in every category *and* statistically significantly different from the intervention group fall scores in every category.

PSYCHOMETRIC PROPERTIES OF THE CLASSROOM OBSERVATION

Like the other parts of the ELLCO Toolkit, Research Edition, the Classroom Observation has been used for research for the NEQRC and LEEP. The Classroom Observation also has been used as a part of a school improvement project in the Philadelphia public school system in classrooms that range from kindergarten through Grade 5. It has also been introduced to school systems in Connecticut and Maine. In these settings, it is being used both to collect data on and to provide a basis for discussions about classroom quality.

The psychometric properties presented in the sections that follow come from various analyses of data from Year 4 of the NEQRC research project combined with data collected from Years 1–3 of the LEEP project. Data from the NEQRC project were collected during the winter of 1998–1999 ($n = 29$). The data from Year 1 of the LEEP project were collected in the fall of 1998 ($n = 27$) and the spring of 1999 ($n = 27$). Data from Year 2 of the LEEP project were collected in the fall of 1999 ($n = 42$) and spring of 2000 ($n = 38$). Data from Year 3 of the LEEP project were collected in the fall of 2000 and spring of 2001 in New England (fall: n = 34; spring: n = 37) and North Carolina (fall: n = 37; spring: n = 37). Together, the projects resulted in a total sample size of 308 classrooms, though the actual subscale size varies depending on the analyses conducted. As with the other parts of the ELLCO Toolkit, the data reported here for the Classroom Observation come from centers and classrooms in lower income communities.

Interrater Reliability

Research use of the Classroom Observation was predicated on appropriate training of observers, as explained in the section of this technical report on the Literacy Environment Checklist. Novice observers' initial observations were conducted with an experienced observer in order to ensure appropriate calibration to the rubrics in the Classroom Observation. When observers were trained and supervised appropriately, we consistently achieved interrater reliabilities of 90% and better for this part of the ELLCO Toolkit.

General Statistics

On the basis of our theoretical beliefs and preliminary analyses of the data, we chose to create three summary variables for the Classroom Observation: the *General Classroom Environment* subtotal; the *Language, Literacy, and Curriculum* subtotal; and the *Total* score. One item (Item 3), Presence and Use of Technology, was problematic[1] and was excluded from all summaries and analyses. Items included in the two subtotals in the ELLCO Toolkit, Research Edition, are as follows.

General Classroom Environment subtotal:

1. Organization of the Classroom

2. Contents of the Classroom

4. Opportunities for Child Choice and Initiative

5. Classroom Management Strategies

6. Classroom Climate

---

[1]By problematic, we mean that scores for Presence and Use of Technology did not cluster with scores for the other items, suggesting that effective use of technology reflects capabilities somewhat distinct from those captured by the other items in the Classroom Observation. In addition the scores for Presence and Use of Technology did not relate clearly to the *General Classroom Environment* subtotal or to the *Language, Literacy, and Curriculum* subtotal; therefore, it was not included in the reported averages or calculations of Cronbach's alpha for the total tool. For this item in 308 classrooms, the mean was 2.45, with a standard deviation of 1.09 and a minimum of 1.0 and a maximum of 5.0.

Language, Literacy, and Curriculum subtotal:

7. Oral Language Facilitation

8. Presence of Books

9P. Approaches to Book Reading (Prekindergarten and Kindergarten Version)

10P. Approaches to Children's Writing (Prekindergarten and Kindergarten Version)

11. Approaches to Curriculum Integration

12. Recognizing Diversity in the Classroom

13. Facilitating Home Support for Literacy

14. Approaches to Assessment

Using these subtotals, we obtained data from classrooms throughout New England that provide some indication of observed levels of performance in classrooms that serve low-income children. As with the Literacy Environment Checklist, many of the classrooms included were in Head Start programs. Tables A.4 and A.5 report descriptive statistics for the Classroom Observation data gathered as part of the NEQRC and LEEP studies (*n* = 308).

Reliability Analysis

Reliability analysis was conducted to examine the internal consistency of the Classroom Observation using data from 308 classrooms. Table A.6 shows the Cronbach's alphas obtained for the two composites, *General Classroom Environment* and *Language, Literacy, and Curriculum*, and for the *Total* score of all of the items on the Classroom Observation that were included in these analyses.

　　Cronbach's alpha of .83 for the *General Classroom Environment* shows good internal consistency for this composite. All of the item–total correlations

Table A.4.　Descriptive statistics for data for the Classroom Observation in the ELLCO Toolkit, Research Edition (*n* = 308)

Composite variable	Mean	Standard deviation	Minimum	Maximum
General Classroom Environment subtotal	3.44	0.79	1.20	5.00
Language, Literacy, and Curriculum subtotal	3.02	0.75	1.13	5.00
Classroom Observation Total score	3.15	0.71	1.29	5.00

Table A.5. Frequencies of classrooms (*n* = 308) with Classroom Observation (ELLCO Toolkit, Research Edition) scores in each of the following categories: *high-quality support* (scores ranging from 3.51 to 5), *basic support* (scores ranging from 2.51 to 3.5), and *low-quality support* (scores less than or equal to 2.5)

Composite variable	High-quality support		Basic support		Low-quality support	
General Classroom Environment subtotal	47.4%	(146)	42.2%	(130)	10.4%	(32)
Language, Literacy, and Curriculum subtotal	24.0%	(74)	45.8%	(141)	30.2%	(93)
Classroom Observation Total score	27.9%	(86)	52.6%	(162)	19.5%	(60)

were high—with correlation coefficients ranging from .60 for Item 1, Organization of the Classroom, to .75 for Item 6, Classroom Climate—with the exception of Item 2, Contents of the Classroom. This item had the lowest item–total correlation, which was nonetheless a moderate correlation (r = .53).

The internal consistency of the *Language, Literacy, and Curriculum* composite is very good, with an alpha of .86. All of the item–total correlations were moderate to high, ranging from .55 for Item 8, Presence of Books, to .65 for Item 13, Facilitating Home Support for Literacy.

Cronbach's alpha of .90 also shows very good internal consistency for all items combined on the Classroom Observation. All of the item–total correlations for the *Classroom Observation Total* were moderate to high (r = .39 to r = .68).

Measuring Stability and Change

Again, in the LEEP project, classrooms were observed in the fall and in the spring of Years 1–3, yielding the ability to measure change over time using the Classroom Observation. Some of the teachers were taking a yearlong course

Table A.6. Cronbach's alpha for data for the Classroom Observation in the ELLCO Toolkit, Research Edition (*n* = 308)

Composite variable	Alpha
General Classroom Environment subtotal	.83
Language, Literacy, and Curriculum subtotal	.86
Classroom Observation Total score	.90

that focused on early language and literacy (our intervention group); the remaining teachers were not (our comparison group). Using data from the comparison group classrooms, we have data on the ability of the Classroom Observation to measure both stability and change over time (see Table A.7).

The two groups began the fall with similar scores on the three dimensions of the Classroom Observation, with the comparison group scores being slightly lower overall, though not statistically significantly lower, than the intervention group scores. In the spring, the comparison group scores remained stable, though slightly higher overall, with no statistically significant changes from fall to spring. As hoped, the LEEP intervention group scores changed significantly from fall to spring in all categories. These changes resulted in intervention group scores that were statistically significantly different from the comparison group scores in every category *and* statistically significantly different from intervention group fall scores in every category.

From our comparison group data, we were able to conclude that the Classroom Observation is able to capture *stability* in classroom quality. This is a good indicator of the Classroom Observation's test–retest reliability. Our data also show that the Classroom Observation is able to capture *changes* in classroom quality associated with a literacy-focused intervention. These findings come from two sources: evidence of fall-to-spring growth and differences between the intervention and comparison groups. These data provide evidence of the *instructional sensitivity* of this tool. The concept of instructional sensitiv-

Table A.7. Stability and change in Classroom Observation scores (ELLCO Toolkit, Research Edition), fall and spring means, for Years 1–3 of the Literacy Environment Enrichment Program (LEEP)

	Fall		Spring	
Composite variable	Comparison group ($n = 65$)	LEEP intervention ($n = 42$)	Comparison group ($n = 65$)	LEEP intervention ($n = 42$)
General Classroom Environment subtotal	3.26	3.61	3.42 ($t = 1.96, p = $ n.s.)	3.91 ($t = 2.26, p < .05$)
Language, Literacy, and Curriculum subtotal	2.85	3.01	2.93 ($t = 1.13, p = $ n.s.)	3.75 ($t = 5.50, p < .0001$)
Classroom Observation *Total* score	2.97	3.19	3.08 ($t = 1.53, p = $ n.s.)	3.74 ($t = 4.88, p < .0001$)

n.s., not significant.

ity is an important factor in determining the quality of research instruments. Our data suggest that the Classroom Observation is both stable and sensitive to interventions that target literacy in ways that are consistent with its assumptions about what constitutes appropriate early literacy practices.

Correlation with Another Widely Used Measure

As part of the NEQRC project, the Classroom Observation has been used in conjunction with the Classroom Profile (Abbott-Shim & Sibley, 1998), a widely used tool for assessing the overall quality of early childhood classrooms. One reason that the Classroom Observation was initially developed was that existing observation tools did not adequately or systematically address early language and literacy experiences or classroom features that are known to support literacy development (Dickinson & Tabors, 2001). Thus, it was our belief that the Classroom Observation would exhibit divergent validity when used in conjunction with these other tools, indicating that it is measuring something qualitatively different. To examine this hypothesis we correlated the *General Classroom Environment* subtotal, the *Language, Literacy, and Curriculum* subtotal, and the *Classroom Observation Total* score with the raw scores from two subscales from the Classroom Profile that we employed, *Learning Environment* and *Scheduling.* We found moderate correlations for all three Classroom Observation variables with scores on the Classroom Profile's *Learning Environment* subscale ($r = .41, .31,$ and $.44$, respectively) but not the profile's *Scheduling* subscale ($r = .12, .09,$ and $.07$, respectively). We take the finding of the modest positive relationship to the Classroom Profile's *Learning Environment* subscale as providing convergent validity for the Classroom Observation. The absence of relationship with the profile's *Scheduling* subscale provides divergent validity because the Classroom Observation was developed to tap a construct that is distinct from that examined by the *Scheduling* subscale.

Predicting Child Outcomes

Possibly the most important test for a tool that purports to evaluate the quality of support provided for children's literacy development is the capacity of the tool to predict children's literacy development. The Classroom Observation has been used in correlational research and employed in hierarchical linear modeling designed to determine the contributions of classroom quality to children's receptive vocabulary (Peabody Picture Vocabulary Test–Third Edition; Dunn & Dunn, 1997) and early literacy scores (Profile of Early Literacy Development; Dickinson & Chaney, 1998). This sophisticated analytic approach allows identification of different sources of variation in children's scores, distinguishing variation between classrooms that is associated with children's backgrounds (e.g., income, gender) from variation associated with their classroom experiences. Level 1 models examining between-group variability took into account variables such as home language (English, Spanish, or other), gender, and age. The variance in scores that was not accounted for by the background factors (15% for vocabulary, 20% for literacy) was attributed to classroom factors. Our models examining sources of classroom-related variance found that scores on the Classroom Observation accounted for 80% of the between-classroom variance in vocabulary and 67% of the between-classroom variance in early literacy (Dickinson et al., 2000). Although revealing the power of the Classroom Observation to predict child outcomes, these analyses also provide evidence that the quality of preschool classrooms attended by children from low-income families can play an important role in supporting their vocabulary growth and early literacy development.

PSYCHOMETRIC PROPERTIES OF THE LITERACY ACTIVITIES RATING SCALE

Like the Classroom Observation and the Literacy Environment Checklist, the Literacy Activities Rating Scale of the ELLCO Toolkit, Research Edition, has been used to conduct research as part of the NEQRC and LEEP, and the data presented here are from centers and classrooms in lower income communities. The psychometric properties presented for the rating scale are based on data from Year 4 of the NEQRC project, combined with data from Years 1–3 of the LEEP project. Data from the NEQRC project were collected during the winter of 1998–1999 ($n = 30$). The data from Year 1 of the LEEP project were collected in the fall of 1998 ($n = 28$) and the spring of 1999 ($n = 528$). Data from Year 2 of the LEEP project were collected in the fall of 1999 ($n = 42$) and spring of 2000 ($n = 40$). Data from Year 3 of the LEEP project were collected in the fall of 2000 ($n = 47$) and spring of 2001 ($n = 47$). Together, the projects resulted in a total sample size of 262, although actual subsample size varies depending on the analyses conducted. As with the Literacy Environment Checklist, the rating scale has been used for research only in preschool classrooms, many of which are in Head Start programs. Some items from the Literacy Activities Rating Scale have been incorporated into the ELLCO Pre-K and have informed the development of the ELLCO K–3, but there is no Literacy Activities Rating Scale in the ELLCO Pre-K or K–3.

Interrater Reliability

Observers underwent a training process explained in the section of this technical report that describes interrater reliability for the Literacy Environment Checklist and the Classroom Observation. As with those parts of the ELLCO Toolkit, Research Edition, novice observers' initial observations were conducted with an experienced observer. Because the Literacy Activities Rating Scale was used simply to describe activities observed during the classroom visit, we did not maintain formal records of interrater reliability. Observers who visited classrooms together, however, had little difficulty arriving at the same ratings for the classrooms they visited. When observers were trained and supervised appropriately, we achieved an average interrater reliability of 81% with relative ease.

General Statistics

On the basis of our theoretical beliefs and preliminary analyses of the data, we created three summary variables for the Literacy Activities Rating Scale: the *Full-Group Book Reading* subtotal, the *Writing* subtotal, and the *Total* score. The *Total* score includes all but two items, which were problematic: Item 4 ("Did you observe an adult engaged in one-to-one book reading or small-group book reading?") and Item 5 ("Is time set aside for children to look at books alone or with a friend?"). These two items were excluded from all analyses. The *Full-Group Book Reading* subtotal includes Items 1–3, which address the number of book reading sessions observed, the length of time spent on full-group book reading, and the total number of books read. The *Writing* subtotal includes Items 6–9, which catalog any observations of children writing as well as any instances of adults assisting children with or modeling writing. Table A.8 reports descriptive statistics for Literacy Activities Rating Scale data gathered as part of the NEQRC and LEEP studies ($n = 262$).

Table A.8.   Descriptive statistics for data for the Literacy Activities Rating Scale in the ELLCO Toolkit, Research Edition ($n = 262$)

Composite variable	Mean	Standard deviation	Minimum	Maximum
Full-Group Book Reading subtotal	2.86	1.95	0	6.00
Writing subtotal	2.10	1.39	0	5.00
Literacy Activities Rating Scale Total score	5.80	2.63	0	13.00

Reliability Analysis

Reliability analysis was conducted to examine the internal consistency of the Literacy Activities Rating Scale. Table A.9 shows the alphas obtained for the *Total* score (excluding the two problematic items mentioned previously), as well as the two subtotals. Cronbach's alpha of .66 for the *Total* score shows somewhat low but acceptable internal consistency for this measure. Item–total correlations ranged from a low of .17 for Item 9 ("Did an adult model writing?") to a high of .49 for Item 1 ("How many full-group book-reading sessions did you observe?").

Cronbach's alpha of .92 for the *Full-Group Book Reading* subtotal shows excellent internal consistency for this composite. All item–total correlations were high ($r = .79$ to $r = .88$). The Cronbach's alpha for the *Writing* subtotal was .73, indicating good internal consistency. Item–total correlations were moderate to high, ranging from a low of .37 for Item 9 ("Did an adult model writing?") to a high of .64 for Item 7 ("Did you see children attempting to write letters or words?"). Given the stronger psychometric properties of the two subscales, we advise using the scores on the distinct subscales of the Literacy Activities Rating Scale instead of the total score when analyzing data from this part of the ELLCO Toolkit, Research Edition.

Measuring Stability and Change

Given the data collected from the LEEP classrooms, we have reported preliminary findings on the ability of the Literacy Activities Rating Scale to measure both stability and change over time (see Table A.10). To determine the stability of the Literacy Activities Rating Scale, we examined the fall and spring scores of the comparison group and LEEP intervention classrooms. We noted that on the *Total* score and the *Full-Group Book Reading* subtotal, the intervention group showed no significant change but that it did show significant change on the *Writing* subtotal. In contrast, the comparison group showed sig-

Table A.9. Cronbach's alpha for data for the Literacy Activities Rating Scale in the ELLCO Toolkit, Research Edition ($n = 262$)

Composite variable	Alpha
Full-Group Book Reading subtotal	.92
Writing subtotal	.73
Literacy Activities Rating Scale Total score	.66

Table A.10. Stability and change in Literacy Activities Rating Scale scores (ELLCO Toolkit, Research Edition), fall and spring means, for Years 1 and 2 of the Literacy Environment Enrichment Program (LEEP)

Composite variable	Fall		Spring	
	Comparison group ($n = 38$)	LEEP intervention ($n = 53$)	Comparison group ($n = 38$)	LEEP intervention ($n = 53$)
Full-Group Book Reading subtotal	2.13	2.79	1.47 ($t = -2.07, p < .05$)	2.89 ($t = 0.28, p = $ n.s.)
Writing subtotal	1.57	2.17	2.16 ($t = 2.81, p < .01$)	2.68 ($t = 2.18, p < .05$)
Literacy Activities Rating Scale score	4.70	5.73	4.70 ($t = 0, p = $ n.s.)	6.68 ($t = 1.94, p = $ n.s.)

n.s., not significant.

nificant changes on both subtotals but not on the *Total* score. We concluded that the Book Reading portion of the Literacy Activities Rating Scale and the overall scale are reasonably stable but that the Writing portion may be relatively more labile, possibly reflecting the developmental changes that occur as children gain literacy skill over the course of the year. Evidence of the *instructional sensitivity* of the Literacy Activities Rating Scale comes from data for the LEEP intervention approach, which we noted reflected significant fall-to-spring change on all dimensions.

CORRELATIONS AMONG THE ELLCO TOOLKIT (RESEARCH EDITION) MEASURES

In Table A.11, we report correlations among the three measures that make up the ELLCO Toolkit, Research Edition. The variables included in these analyses are as follows:

- The *Books* subtotal, the *Writing* subtotal, the *Literacy Environment Checklist Total*

- The *Language, Literacy, and Curriculum* subtotal; the *General Classroom Environment subtotal;* and the *Classroom Observation Total*

- The *Full-Group Book Reading* subtotal, the *Writing* subtotal, and the *Literacy Activities Rating Scale Total*

Table A.11. Correlations for data from New England Quality Research Center (NEQRC) Year 4 and Literacy Environment Enrichment Program (LEEP) Years 1 and 2 (n = 92)

Composite variable	Literacy Environment Checklist			Classroom Observation			Literacy Activities Rating Scale	
	1	2	3	4	5	6	7	8
1. Literacy Environment Checklist: Books	—							
2. Literacy Environment Checklist: Writing	.62***	—						
3. Literacy Environment Checklist Total	.89***	.90***	—					
4. Classroom Observation: General Classroom Environment	.47***	.51***	.53***	—				
5. Classroom Observation: Language, Literacy, and Curriculum	.65***	.64***	.69***	.69***	—			
6. Classroom Observation Total	.62***	.63***	.67***	.87***	.95***	—		
7. Literacy Activities Rating Scale: Full-Book Reading	.10	.11	.11	.06	.14*	.11	—	
8. Literacy Activities Rating Scale: Writing	.36***	.43***	.43***	.37***	.47***	.46***	.04	—
9. Literacy Activities Rating Scale Total	.33***	.37***	.38***	.31***	.44***	.41***	.75***	.63***

$*p < .05$ $**p < .01$ $***p < .001$

We found that the *Language, Literacy, and Curriculum* subtotal and *the General Classroom Environment* subtotal are highly correlated with the *Classroom Observation Total* (r = .95 and .87, respectively) though not as highly with each other (r = .69). This modest correlation between the two subscales of the Classroom Observation provides support for the fact that the two subscales should be examined separately.

In addition, there are moderate-to-strong correlations for all three Classroom Observation variables with both the *Books* subtotal (r = .65, .47, and .62, respectively) and the *Writing subtotal* (r = .64, .51, and .63, respectively) of the Literacy Environment Checklist. The *Literacy Environment Checklist Total* exhibits an even stronger relationship with the Classroom Observation scores (r = .69, .67, and .53, respectively). The *Books* and *Writing* subtotals for the checklist are highly correlated with the *Literacy Environment Checklist Total* (r = .89 and .90, respectively), but not as highly correlated with each other (r = .62).

The *Literacy Activities Rating Scale Total* score and the *Writing* subtotal for the rating scale are moderately related to the three Classroom Observation scores (r = .44, .31, and .41, respectively, and r = .47, .37, and .46, respectively). Although the *Full-Group Book Reading* subtotal does not show a statistically significant relationship to the *Classroom Observation Total* score (r = .11) or the *General Classroom Environment* subtotal (r = .06), there is a statistically significant correlation between the *Full-Group Book Reading* subtotal and the *Language, Literacy, and Curriculum* subtotal. The *Literacy Activities Rating Scale Total* score and the *Writing* subtotal are moderately correlated with all three Literacy Environment Checklist scores (r = .33, .38, and .37, respectively, and r = .36, .43, and .43, respectively). The rating scale's *Full-Group Book Reading* and *Writing* subtotals are both highly correlated with the *Literacy Activities Rating Scale Total* score (r = .75 and r = .63, respectively) yet are not statistically significantly correlated with one another, indicating that the two subscales are measuring different constructs.

ADDENDUM

Cronbach's alpha analyses parallel to those described thus far were performed using a larger sample (n = 646) of data collected with the ELLCO Toolkit, Research Edition, between 2002 and 2007. These data come from the following sources:

- The New England Quality Research Center: The Next Generation (2001–2006, n = 182)

- Examining the Efficacy of Two Models of Preschool Professional Development in Language and Literacy (2005–2007, n = 213)

- Child Care Quality: Does Partnership Make a Difference: An Extension of the Partnership Impact Project (2004–2007, $n = 66$)

- Evaluation of the Newport Early Reading First Collaborative (2003–2006, $n = 66$)

- Evaluation of the Springfield Early Reading First Initiative (2003–2007, $n = 66$)

- Connecticut Is Reading First (2005–2007, $n = 53$)

Results of the Cronbach's alpha analyses, described in detail next for each section of the ELLCO Toolkit, Research Edition, corroborate the other findings reported in this technical report and thereby strengthen confidence in the internal reliability of the tool.

Alpha coefficients for the *Literacy Environment Checklist Total* score as well as the *Books* and *Writing* subtotals all show good internal consistency (see Table A.12). Item–total correlations for the *Books* subtotal were moderate, ranging from .23 to .59. Item–total correlations for the *Writing* subtotal also were moderate ($r = .23$ to $r = .53$), with the exception of Item 13 ("Is an alphabet visible?") and Item 24 ("Are there puzzles with words available for children's use?") ($r = .17$ for both). Those two items also exhibited low item–total correlation with the *Literacy Environment Checklist Total* score ($r = .13$ and .16, respectively), whereas the remaining items displayed moderate ($r = .21$ to $r = .57$) item–total correlation with the total score.

The Cronbach's alpha coefficients for the *General Classroom Environment* subtotal, the *Language, Literacy, and Curriculum* subtotal and the *Classroom Observation Total* score all show good to excellent internal consistency (Table A.13). Furthermore, both of the Classroom Observation subtotals as well as the *Total* score exhibited moderate to high item–total correlations, ranging from .57 to .73 for the *General Classroom Environment* subscale, .60 to .73 for the *Language, Literacy, and Curriculum* subscale, and .56 to .77 for the *Total* score.

In Table A.14, the *Full-Group Book Reading* alpha of .90 shows very good internal consistency for this subtotal. The *Writing* subtotal and *Literacy Activities Rating Scale Total* score both show good internal consistency with alphas

Table A.12. Cronbach's alpha for larger sample data (2001–2007) for the Literacy Environment Checklist in the ELLCO Toolkit, Research Edition ($n = 616$)

Composite variable	Alpha
Books subtotal	.76
Writing subtotal	.75
Literacy Environment Checklist Total score	.84

Table A.13. Cronbach's alpha for larger sample data (2001–2007) for the Classroom Observation in the ELLCO Toolkit, Research Edition (*n* = 634)

Composite variable	Alpha
General Classroom Environment subtotal	.84
Language, Literacy, and Curriculum subtotal	.89
Classroom Observation Total score	.93

of .74 and .72, respectively. Item–total correlations for the *Full-Group Book Reading* subscale were high, ranging from .75 to .85. The items that compose the *Writing* subtotal showed moderate to high item–total correlations of .47 to .64. The *Literacy Activities Rating Scale Total* score also had moderate to high item–total correlations that ranged from .30 to .56.

On the basis of the psychometric properties of the ELLCO Toolkit, Research Edition, as well as the theoretical and practical considerations outlined in Chapter 1, we revised the ELLCO to include more specificity, in the form of detailed descriptive indicators for each scale point, as well as a broader range of measures of quality in early literacy, such as phonological awareness, efforts to build vocabulary, opportunities for extended conversations, and environmental print in the ELLCO Pre-K. Although the ELLCO Pre-K is more thorough and expansive than the Research Edition, it does include the same content covered by the earlier version, with the exception of Research Edition Item 3, Presence and Use of Technology. Cronbach's alpha analyses on the ELLCO Toolkit, Research Edition, described earlier in this technical report, indicated that this construct was not statistically related to the other items; therefore, it was not included in the ELLCO Pre-K or K–3.

Users of the ELLCO K–3 who are familiar with the ELLCO Toolkit, Research Edition, will notice that there is now less emphasis on teacher responses to the Teacher Interview, which, in the Research Edition, informed scoring decisions for several items (e.g., Item 13, Facilitation of Home Support for Literacy; Item 14, Approaches to Assessment). Aspects of these and other items from the original toolkit have now been integrated with items in the K–3 ver-

Table A.14. Cronbach's alpha for larger sample data (2001–2007) for the Literacy Activities Rating Scale in the ELLCO Toolkit, Research Edition (*n* = 547)

Composite variable	Alpha
Full-Group Book Reading subtotal	.90
Writing subtotal	.74
Literacy Activities Rating Scale total score	.72

sion. All items are now based predominantly on observable classroom indicators to increase validity and reliability.

In conclusion, the psychometric data collected and analyzed for the original ELLCO Toolkit, Research Edition, has been instrumental to the development of both the ELLCO Pre-K and the newly created ELLCO K–3. Direct comparison of the original ELLCO Toolkit to the ELLCO K–3 is not possible, nor would it be appropriate, as there is currently no data for the ELLCO K–3. However, the structural features that have been retained, along with the added depth and breadth of content relevant to reading and writing instruction in the primary grades, leads to the hope that the ELLCO K–3 will prove to be as strong and reliable a tool as the original ELLCO Toolkit that inspired it.

REFERENCES

Abbott-Shim, M., & Sibley, A. (1998). *Assessment Profile for Early Childhood Programs.* Atlanta, GA: Quality Assist.

Dickinson, D.K., & Chaney, C. (1998). *Profile of Early Literacy Development.* Newton, MA: Education Development Center, Inc.

Dickinson, D.K., Sprague, K., Sayer, A., Miller, C., Clark, N., & Wolf, A. (2000). Classroom factors that foster literacy and social development of children from different language backgrounds. In M. Hopman (Chair), *Dimensions of program quality that foster child development: Reports from 5 years of the Head Start Quality Research Centers.* Poster session presented at the biannual National Head Start Research Conference, Washington, DC.

Dickinson, D.K., & Tabors, P.O. (Eds.). (2001). *Beginning literacy with language: Young children learning at home and school.* Baltimore: Paul H. Brookes Publishing Co.

Dunn, L.M., & Dunn, L.M. (1997). *Peabody Picture Vocabulary Test–Third Edition.* Circle Pines, MN: American Guidance Service.

Smith, M.W., Brady, J.P., & Anastasopoulos, L. (2008). *Early Language and Literacy Classroom Observation Tool, Pre-K* (ELLCO Pre-K). Baltimore: Paul H. Brookes Publishing Co.

Smith, M.W., & Dickinson, D.K. (with Sangeorge, A., & Anastasopoulos, L.). (2002a). *Early Language and Literacy Classroom Observation Toolkit* (Research ed.). Baltimore: Paul H. Brookes Publishing Co.

Smith, M.W., & Dickinson, D.K. (with Sangeorge, A., & Anastasopoulos, L.). (2002b). *User's Guide to the Early Language and Literacy Classroom Observation Toolkit* (Research ed.). Baltimore: Paul H. Brookes Publishing Co.

Resources

WEB SITES

American Library Association Book Lists

http://www.ala.org/ala/alsc/alscresources/booklists/booklists.htm

The American Library Association seeks to promote high-quality library and information services. This web site provides parents, teachers, and child care providers with book lists for children, with different lists based around ages, cultural backgrounds, and themes. Following are two lists of particular relevance.

ALA Bilingual Books for Children

http://www.ala.org/ala/alsc/alscresources/booklists/bilingualbooks.htm

This list compiles books for children from birth to age 14. Each book has bilingual text, and the list is organized by language. Books with text in 12 different languages are included, with an extensive section on books with Spanish text.

ALA Suggested Books

http://www.ala.org/ala/alsc/alscresources/booklists/suggestedbooks.htm

This region provides a book list that was compiled by a Reading Is Fundamental committee. The list is organized by age group and provides titles and author information on recommended books for children birth to age 14.

Aspectos Culturales

http://www.aspectosculturales.com

This web site aims to improve cultural awareness in children and adults and improve the understanding and use of the Spanish language by teachers, children, and other adults. It provides teachers and other adults with resources and ideas for raising their awareness of Hispanic language and culture, as well as strategies for how to incorporate this awareness into the classroom. Ideas for books, games, music, resources, and activities geared at building awareness and integration are included.

¡Colorín Colorado!

http://www.colorincolorado.org

A web-based service of the Reading Rockets project, ¡Colorín Colorado! provides information, activities, and advice for educators and Spanish-speaking families of English language learners. The information on ¡Colorín Colorado! (in English and in Spanish) is based on a combination of direct research, expert opinion, and recommended practice.

International Reading Association

http://www.reading.org

The International Reading Association (IRA) is a professional organization for individuals involved in teaching reading. The organization's web site provides membership information; links to key publications of the IRA; a list of useful web resources including lesson plans, booklists, and parent resources; an online store; and links to other relevant and important web sites for reading teachers.

Literacy Coaching Clearinghouse

http://www.literacycoachingonline.org

The Literacy Coaching Clearinghouse is a joint venture of the International Reading Association and the National Council of Teachers of English. Its mission is to "increase the knowledge base, research, and practice of literacy coaching." This web site provides an overview of literacy coaching, a set of brief publications, a more extensive list of collected key resources, a section on literacy coaching programs, links to key organizations in literacy coaching, a literacy coaching blog, and postings about events that might be of interest to practitioners.

National Association for the Education of Young Children (NAEYC)

http://www.naeyc.org

NAEYC is the world's largest organization working in the interest of children birth through age 8. Its focus is on ensuring that all young children receive quality educational and developmental services. It has a network of several hundred state and local affiliates dedicated to pursuing its mission. NAEYC's web site provides important information on accreditation, conferences, membership, public policy, and early childhood.

National Center for Family Literacy

http://www.famlit.org

The National Center for Family Literacy seeks to use the power inherent in families to help solve the literacy crisis. The center creates and funds initiatives across the United States, some of which target children from diverse backgrounds, which support family literacy, and which promote the joint role of parents and teachers in fostering literacy in children. The web site describes the center's mission and methods and provides information for parents and teachers on how they can benefit from the center's work.

National Institute for Literacy

http://nifl.gov

The National Institute for Literacy is a federal agency that provides leadership and information on literacy issues. The institute is especially focused on improving language and literacy instruction for children and adults. The web site provides information and downloadable guides on language and literacy development and instruction for both teachers and parents.

PBS Parents Web Site

http://www.pbs.org/parents

The PBS Parents web site is hosted by PBS and provides games, activities, and parenting advice for parents of children of all ages. The web site provides parent and child care providers with guides on child development, children and media, creativity, early math, going to school, raising boys, reading and language, and talking with children. The following three regions of the web site are particularly relevant.

Bookfinder

http://www.pbs.org/parents/bookfinder

The PBS Parents Bookfinder region provides parents and child care providers with a search engine for age-appropriate, high-quality children's books. The search can be conducted by age, book theme, or specific search terms and includes a list of high-quality books with author information and book descriptions. The search also includes Spanish-language books.

Creativity

http://www.pbs.org/parents/creativity

The PBS Parents Creativity region is a set of online tools and activities designed to help parents explore creativity with their children. Activities include simple games and ideas for offline activities that foster children's intellectual engagement.

Reading/Language

http://www.pbs.org/parents/readinglanguage

The PBS Parents Reading/Language region provides parents with research-based information on reading and language development from birth to third grade. It presents milestones for each age, as well as key strategies for helping children of that age with appropriate language and learning support as they develop their emergent literacy skills.

Reading Is Fundamental—Leamos en familia!

http://www.rif.org/leer

This Spanish version of the Reading Is Fundamental web site provides ideas and activities for families to explore reading in their everyday lives. The web site is organized around different rooms in a house, which function as themes around which activities are structured.

Reading Rockets

http://www.readingrockets.org

Reading Rockets is a multimedia project that provides information on how children learn to read and resources to help parents and educators support literacy development. The web site has pages that offer techniques for teaching children to read, strategies for helping struggling readers, and a search tool for recommended books for young children. In addition, the web site houses multimedia resources, including videos, webcasts, and podcasts about early literacy development, as well as links to other resources. Reading Rockets has an affiliated Spanish–English bilingual web site, ¡Colorín Colorado! (http://www.colorincolorado.org; described previously in this resources list).

read • write • think

http://www.readwritethink.org

This web site is a partnership between the International Reading Association (IRA), the National Council of Teachers of English (NCTE), and the Verizon Foundation and provides teachers with effective practices and resources in reading and language arts instruction. A major highlight of this is the wide array of standards-based lesson plans that integrate technology into instruction and learning.

Scientific Council on the Developing Child

http://www.developingchild.net

The Scientific Council on the Developing Child is a multidisciplinary organization whose mission is to bridge the gap between the science of early child development and public decision making and policy. The web site provides an overview of the council's work as well as downloadable documents and links to key council publications.

WEB RESOURCES

Put Reading First: Helping Your Child Learn to Read. Parent Guide: Preschool Through Grade 3

http://www.nifl.gov/partnershipforreading/publications/Parent_br.pdf

This downloadable parent guide gives a short overview of the National Reading Panel findings and provides suggestions for what to expect from a school reading program based on scientific research. The guide ends with a section on how parents can reinforce their children's early literacy development with activities and games in the home.

ReadingQuest

http://readingquest.org

Teachers will find a wide assortment of strategies for reading comprehension on this site. Most of the strategies are accompanied by handouts or blackline masters that can be downloaded or printed out for classroom use.

Teaching That Makes Sense

http://www.ttms.org

The web site provides an array of documents for teachers that can be used for instruction and professional development in the areas of reading and writing. Downloadable documents include *What is Good Writing?; Welcome to Writer's Workshop;* and *Read Like a Reader; Read Like a Writer.* The materials are well written and visually appealing.

What Is Scientifically Based Research? A Guide for Teachers

http://www.nifl.gov/partnershipforreading/publications/science_research.pdf

This teacher-oriented guide provides a quick overview of what scientifically based research is and why it is important in instructional design. It provides a basic summary of how scientific evaluation research works and suggestions for how research can be translated into classroom practice.

RESEARCH ARTICLES, BOOKS, AND BOOK CHAPTERS

Ada, A.F. (2003). *A magical encounter: Latino children's literature in the classroom* (2nd ed.). Boston: Allyn & Bacon.

This book is a wonderful resource for building a multicultural library and provides teachers a wealth of ideas for infusing Latino literature into their classrooms. Moreover, there are practical suggestions that teachers can apply to any text or teaching context.

Beck, I.L., McKeown, & Kucan, L. (2002). *Bringing words to life: Robust vocabulary instruction.* New York: Guilford Press.

Through a research-based framework, strategies for effective vocabulary instruction are clearly presented in the book. Aimed at educators teaching the very youngest children up through high school, this book offers rich information about how to choose words to teach and how to create an exciting, word-loving environment.

Biemiller, A. (2006). Vocabulary development and instruction: A prerequisite for school learning. In D.K. Dickinson & S.B. Neuman (Eds.), *Handbook of early literacy research* (Vol. 2, pp. 41–51). New York: Guilford Press.

This chapter discusses the important links between early vocabulary and later literacy. It discusses the scientific evidence for this link, emphasizing the size and sequence of vocabulary development and the importance of acquiring word meaning. Finally, it discusses practical implications of this research for teachers in classroom settings.

Bowman, B. (Ed.). (2002). *Love to read: Essays in developing and enhancing early literacy skills of African American children*. Washington, DC: National Black Child Development Institute.

This collection of essays arises out of a growing concern about the disparity in literacy and school performance between African American and Caucasian children. These essays, collected from leading scholars in early literacy education, address pertinent issues ranging from the social and economic causes for this performance gap, to scientific evidence for best literacy practices, to suggestions for how best to help enhance African American children's early literacy skills at an early age.

Duke, N.K., & Bennett-Armistead, V.S. (2003). *Reading and writing informational text in the primary grades: Research-based practices.* New York: Scholastic.

This book shows primary-grade teachers how to teach students to read and write informational text. It provides classroom-tested strategies as well as a framework for organizing time and space.

Durkin, D. (1979). What classroom observations reveal about reading comprehension instruction. *Reading Research Quarterly, 14,* 481–533.

This seminal piece of early research focused attention on reading comprehension. Because Durkin and her team found virtually no reading comprehension instruction occurring in classrooms, research then turned to identifying effective strategies.

Farstrup, A.E., & Samuels, S.J. (2002). *What research has to say about reading instruction* (3rd ed.). Newark, DE: International Reading Association.

The chapters in this book reflect the most current research and policy work in the area of reading and present a balanced blend of theory, basic research, and effective classroom practice.

Gillespie, J.T. (2002). *Best books for children—preschool through grade 6* (7th ed.). Westport, CT: Libraries Unlimited.

This book is an encyclopedic list of books for children of all ages, organized by type of book (e.g., space exploration, picture books). It provides age recommendations, publisher information, and one-sentence descriptions of each of the more than 20,000 books it lists.

Harvey, S., & Goudvis, A. (2000). *Strategies that work: Teaching comprehension to enhance understanding.* York, ME: Stenhouse.

Teachers are provided with practical suggestions to help students think when they read. The authors provide guidance on how to choose texts, how to model strategies, and how to provide students with the opportunity to practice reading comprehension strategies such as asking questions, visualizing, and making inferences and connections.

International Reading Association. (2003). *Evidence-based reading instruction: Putting the National Reading Panel Report into practice.* Newark, DE: Author.

This book is a compendium of articles from International Reading Association journals that specifically address the five components of reading instruction identified by the National Reading Panel: phonemic awareness, phonics, fluency, vocabulary development, and comprehension. The book is written for educators to assist them in implementing these components in the early grades.

Opitz, M.F. (2000). *Rhymes and reasons: Literature and language play for phonological awareness.* Portsmouth, NH: Heinemann.

This book provides an alternative to phonics-based reading instruction, based on various types of language play that facilitate phonological awareness. It provides a detailed guide to various aspects of phonological awareness and ideas for types of activities, games, and free-play that promote it. Finally, the book includes a list of more than 350 books featuring language play and other activities that can be read aloud to facilitate language development.

Opitz, M.F., & Rasinksi, T.V. (1998). *Good-bye round robin: 25 effective oral reading strategies.* Portsmouth, NH: Heinemann.

This practical book presents an assortment of effective techniques teachers can use for oral reading. The book is very easy to read and does a nice job articulating the place for oral reading in a comprehensive reading program.

Ray, K.W. (1999). *Wondrous words: Writers writing in the elementary classroom.* Urbana, IL: NCTE.

This book is a wonderful blend of theory, practice, and classroom vignettes that highlight how students can learn to write from their reading. The author provides teachers with rich descriptions about how to develop the ability to "read like a writer" in their students.

Raphael, T.E., Pardo, L.S., & Highfield, K. (2002). *Book club: A literature-based curriculum* (2nd ed.). Lawrence, MA: Small Planet Communications.

This book provides clear guidance on how to use student-led discussion groups to promote reading, writing, speaking, and listening skills. The authors provide teaching tips, examples of student work, and detailed teaching units.

Rasinski, T.V. (2003). *The fluent reader: Oral reading strategies for building word recognition, fluency, and comprehension.* New York: Scholastic.

The author provides a clear, research-based rationale for oral reading and offers a variety of engaging classroom techniques, ranging from repeated reading to reader's theater.

Snow, C.E., Burns, M.S., & Griffin, P. (Eds.). (1998). *Preventing reading difficulties in young children.* Washington, DC: National Academies Press.

The book summarizes the findings of the Committee on the Prevention of Reading Difficulties in Young Children and explores how to foster literacy from birth through the primary grades in order to prevent children from falling behind in the acquisition of reading.

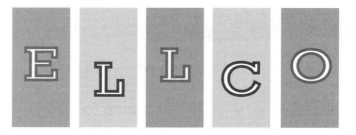

Also available—ELLCO for Pre-K!

By Miriam W. Smith, Ed.D., Joanne P. Brady, M.Ed., & Louisa Anastasopoulos, M.P.P.

ELLCO K-3 users—now there's a dedicated pre-K edition of *ELLCO* designed to *specifically* assess literacy practices and supports in preschool classrooms.

Set up like the K-3 version, *ELLCO Pre-K* has just two parts: a classroom observation to gather critical information about 5 key elements of the literacy environment, and a teacher interview, which supplements the observation with educators' firsthand reflections. This pre-K edition also

- is **validated**—the technical appendix provides all of the research and field-testing updates since the first edition of *ELLCO* was published

- prompts users to look for **preliteracy activities** like storybook reading, circle time conversations, and child-originated storywriting

- includes **preschool-specific descriptors** that show users what to look for during all 5 parts of the observation

- gives complete information about **conducting classroom observations, scoring accurately,** and **limiting bias**

With the pre-K edition of the trusted assessment tool, preschools will have the information they need to determine the effectiveness of their classroom environment, strengthen the quality of programs and teaching practices, and improve young children's early literacy outcomes.